Theodore Dwight Woolsey

The Prometheus of Æschylus

With Notes, for the use of Colleges in the United States

Theodore Dwight Woolsey

The Prometheus of Æschylus
With Notes, for the use of Colleges in the United States

ISBN/EAN: 9783744764087

Printed in Europe, USA, Canada, Australia, Japan

Cover: Foto ©Paul-Georg Meister /pixelio.de

More available books at **www.hansebooks.com**

FIRST LESSONS
ON
NATURAL PHILOSOPHY.

PART FIRST.

WM. JAS. HAMERSLEY has recently published a new stereotype edition of this popular work.

This Book was prepared by the author to meet a want, which she felt in her own experience as a teacher.

It was at that time doubted by many, whether the principles of natural philosophy could be made clear to the minds of young children.

The remarkable simplicity of style, clearness of statement, and aptness of illustration, which characterize this book have entirely removed those doubts.

This little work is used in all parts of the United States; it has received the cordial approbation of parents and teachers, and is a great favorite with pupils.

No text book on natural science, has ever been more thoroughly adapted to the object for which it was written.

The information this book conveys with wonderful tact to the mind of a child, concerning many interesting and important facts and laws of natural philosophy renders it far easier for the scholar, at a later age, to comprehend the more advanced treatise giving instruction in the same science.

The Publisher believes that this and the second part have proved to be important contributions to the cause of education.

OUTLINES OF
ANCIENT AND MODERN HISTORY:

ON A NEW PLAN.

EMBRACING BIOGRAPHICAL NOTICES OF ILLUSTRIOUS PERSONS,

AND GENERAL VIEWS OF THE GEOGRAPHY, POPULATION, POLITICS, RELIGION, MILITARY AND NAVAL AFFAIRS, ARTS, LITERATURE, MANNERS AND CUSTOMS OF ANCIENT AND MODERN NATIONS, WITH QUESTIONS. NEW EDITION.

BY ROYAL ROBBINS.

This is one of the most popular text-books on General History ever published in this country: its extensive and permanent sale attests the estimation in which it is held by teachers. As a clear and comprehensive compend of History it is unsurpassed by any work.

A. Parish, Esq., Principal of the Springfield High School, says of it,

"I have used *Robbins' Outlines of History* constantly, during the last fifteen years; and, although repeatedly solicited to exchange it for other treatises on the same subject, I have not yet satisfied myself that any other work possesses on the whole so many excellencies as this. The style is plain, the subjects are closely stated, and the multitude of interesting facts relating to distinguished men and remarkable events, always impart interest to the study. I regard it as a most excellent work."

J. N. Teruilliger, Esq., Principal of Select English School, Anderson, Ind.,

"I find it as accurate in its facts and dates as it is accurate, clear, and concise in its language. Its style and arrangement are just what they should be for such a work."

W. H. Bannister, Esq., Principal of the Hudson River Institute, Claverack,

"Upon the opening of our Seminary, we introduced *Robbins' Outlines of History* as a text-book, and we find it one of the most complete and suitable works of the kind for advanced classes in this very important study."

Sent by mail prepaid on receipt of the price.

£2.8.6

Campbell

— £2.8.6

THE PROMETHEUS

OF

ÆSCHYLUS,

WITH

NOTES,

FOR

THE USE OF COLLEGES IN THE UNITED STATES.

By THEODORE D. WOOLSEY,

PRESIDENT OF YALE COLLEGE.

NEW EDITION, REVISED.

HARTFORD:
HAMERSLEY & CO.
1869.

GREEK TEXT BOOKS.

WM. JAS. HAMERSLEY, PUBLISHER,

HARTFORD, CONN.

SOPHOCLES' FIRST BOOK IN GREEK, for the use of beginners.

SOPHOCLES' GREEK LESSONS, new edition, adapted to the revised edition of the Author's Greek Grammar.

SOPHOCLES' GREEK GRAMMAR, revised edition, for the use of Schools and Colleges.

SOPHOCLES' GREEK EXERCISES, with an English and Greek vocabulary.

SOPHOCLES' GREEK GRAMMAR, for the use of learners, being the *first* edition of the Author's Grammar.

FELTON'S GREEK READER, containing selections in Prose and Poetry, with Notes and a Lexicon adapted to the Greek Grammar of E. A. Sophocles, by C. C. Felton.

THE ANTIGONE OF SOPHOCLES, with notes, by Theodore D. Woolsey; new edition, revised.

THE ALCESTIS OF EURIPIDES, with notes, by Theodore D. Woolsey; new edition.

THE PROMETHEUS OF ÆSCHYLUS, with notes, by Theodore D. Woolsey; revised edition.

THE ELECTRA OF SOPHOCLES, with notes, by Theodore D. Woolsey; revised edition.

THE GORGIAS OF PLATO, chiefly according to Stallbaum's text, with notes by Theodore D. Woolsey, new edition with additions.

ENTERED according to Act of Congress, in the year 1850, by
JAMES MUNROE AND COMPANY,
in the Clerk's Office of the District Court of the District of Massachusetts.

ENTERED according to Act of Congress, in the year 1869, by
HAMERSLEY AND COMPANY,
in the Clerk's Office of the District Court of the District of Connecticut.

PREFACE.

THE subject of this tragedy is a struggle between absolute power and the spirit of freedom as displayed by an unsubdued will amid the severest sufferings. Prometheus is condemned by the ruler of the Gods to atone for having stolen fire from heaven, by being nailed and chained to a lonely rock. There can be but little action in such a plot where the chief character is passive; but the poet has thrown into it a very deep interest by the person of the sufferer and the grandeur of the scenery, while the few incidents of the play tend directly or by contrast to manifest the unconquerable will of Prometheus. His offence itself enlists our sympathies; it is, that he raised the human race from the lowest misery, against the will of a monarch who sought to destroy it. He is a divinity, and the chief of the allies through whose aid Jupiter tore the sceptre from his father's hand; and by his prophetic spirit he looks through long ages of torture to the time when he is destined to be loosed. Thus, though powerless, he is not in despair; but alive as he is to the feeling of pain, and bewailing, as he does, his lot, he can yet make up his mind to come to no terms with his oppressor, and already triumphs in the prospect that Jupiter will be forced, for his own sake, to set him free.

The play opens with the preparatives for the torture.

Force and Might, two giant ministers of Jove, (see Hesiod's Theogony, 385,) accompanied by Vulcan, appear upon the stage; Force is a mute spectator, and his office may be conceived to have been that of dragging the struggling God to the place. But Might oversees the fulfilment of the sentence; and while Vulcan drives the nails, and clasps the chains, he chides the tardiness of the work, and taunts Prometheus with the folly of his opposition to the Gods. After these executioners have withdrawn, the Chorus of sea-nymphs (probably fifteen in number), hearing the sound of driven steel, assemble and condole with their kinsman: they are the representatives of that honest but weak class, whose open sympathy with the oppressed is beneath the tyrant's notice. Oceanus, their father, next appears, gives wholesome advice to Prometheus, and offers to intercede with Jove in his behalf. The offer is scorned, and indeed was made rather for form's sake, than from any belief that it would be accepted. Oceanus is one who feels a degree of kindness for the oppressed, but wishes mainly to keep himself out of danger, and to stand well with both parties. After his departure, Prometheus, as one who has resolved to endure his evils, and who seeks to occupy his mind with other thoughts, tells the Chorus the blessings which he had conferred upon mankind by the gift of fire. Thus he calls forth our interest, and shows the malignity of Jupiter.

A new sufferer now appears. Io, the victim of lust and vengeance, driven through the wildest parts of the earth in an altered form, passes the spot where Prometheus is chained. He predicts her future course, and relates her past wanderings. She leaves the place, goaded by the same maddening spectre of Argos which drove her thither. The dramatic connection of this part with the rest of the play is somewhat remote. It lies partly in the fact that Prometheus and Io are victims of the same oppression; but chiefly in the decree of fate, that one of her descendants, Hercules, shall loose him from his bonds. But, viewed in regard to internal unity, this part is quite one with the rest, and Io, by the entire contrast of her character in the same circumstances, acts as a foil to Prometheus. *She* is all passive endurance ; *he*, free resistance ; she is despair, and he hope. Even their very woes are contrasted : he, the free one, is chained, and she, the passive one, is left free to wander at large. It must have been the perception of the effect of these contrasts that led the poet, perhaps unconsciously, to select the story of Io from the variety of incidents which he might have woven into the plot.

Prometheus boasts, before Io and the Chorus, that he foresees a ruinous marriage, into which Jupiter will enter, unaware of his danger. Mercury now appears, to demand what marriage he speaks of. He refuses to tell ; and the play closes with a wilder display of vengeance than that with which it opened. The bolt is hurled from heaven ; the elements are thrown into disorder ; the rocks are blasted around Prometheus ; his body is thunder-riven ; but, unyielding still, he cries to the sky and to his mother Themis to behold the injustice which he is suffering. " The triumph of subjection," says Schlegel, " was never celebrated in more glorious strains, and we have difficulty in conceiving how the poet could sustain himself on such an elevation."

It is worthy of remark, that Æschylus in this play seems to scorn the poetical religion of Greece, and to show little reverence towards the chief of the Gods. Elsewhere, and especially in the Choruses of the Suppliants, the character of Jupiter is set forth in terms worthy of the supreme ruler. But here he is the successful usurper, who forgets the friends that helped him ; is a foe to the race of man ;. acts according to his will rather than his reason ; and is controlled by fate. It is not easy to say why so religious a poet ventured to guide his hearer's sympathies against Jupiter and in favor of Prometheus, or how he ventured to choose a plot in which human feelings could take no other channel. One might almost think that he conceived of Jupiter as passing through the changes of character which were to be seen in some Greek tyrants;—as reigning arbitrarily and by force at first, crushing his foes and strengthening his power by whatever means; but afterwards, when his end was gained, becoming mild, just, and the father of Gods and men.* Or it may be that he stood aloof from the pop-

---

* This paragraph of the preface was written for the second edition, in 1840, and the theory here propounded was probably suggested by what Dissen says in Welcker's work, to which reference is made just below. Since that time, in the year 1844, Prof Schömann, of Greifswald, has published his poetical translation of the Prometheus Bound, and a Prometheus Loosed of his own, written with a view to illustrate a theory in regard to the Promethean trilogy. That theory in its outlines is, that we have no right to judge of the final impression of the *tout ensemble* from this play, which formed the middle act of the great drama, and in which Prometheus has the field almost entirely to himself; that the poet did not sympathize with Prometheus, but regarded him as a transgressor of divine law justly punished; and that, in the closing act, where he was freed from his chains by the clemency of Zeus, he owned his fault, submitted, and was heartily reconciled. As for the human sympathies which he enlists by his resistance, on behalf of mankind, to the plans of Zeus, he misrepresents the feelings of Zeus toward the human race, and his intervention is uncalled for. In short, he is partial in his statements, a $\sigma o \phi \iota \sigma \tau \grave{\eta} s$ in a worse sense than that in which Hermes applies to him the term, as well as $\pi \iota \kappa \rho o \hat{\imath} s$ $\hat{\upsilon} \pi \acute{\epsilon} \rho \pi \iota \kappa \rho o s$ (v. 944). The closing member of the trilogy must have purified the minds of the audience from the impressions which the Prometheus Loosed by itself is calculated to make.

It would be idle, within the limits of a note, to discuss this theory, which, proceeding as it did from an admirable scholar, made quite a sensation, and yet failed to work conviction in many minds, and, I must confess, in my own. It defends the religious consistency of Æschylus at the expense of his dramatic skill; for what ought to be said of the art of a poet who, through one whole drama, gives no sign that he does not regard Zeus as acting tyrannically? No character in the piece takes side against Prometheus, except Hermes, the "runner" of

ular religion, and thought it right to use its fables in his dramas with little scruple as to their tendency, while yet his own idea of God was a lofty one, and was inculcated wher-

---

Zeus, and Kratos, who has no more of the moral person about him than a thunderbolt. The Chorus, indeed, pronounce that he has made a mistake in helping mankind (v. 260), and exhort him to greater moderation of language and feeling (vv. 928, 936, 1036); but then they show all along a tender compassion for him, and are willing to share his woes (vv. 1066-1070), as those of an injured person whose side they have espoused. Their father, Oceanus, urges Prometheus to a milder and more yielding course, not because he has sinned, but because a "rough monarch and an irresponsible bears sway." As for Io, it is not easy to see why she is drawn into the stream of the action, unless to increase the tide of feeling against Zeus. And what is most worthy of notice, the words of Hephæstus himself, own son of Zeus, are to his disadvantage: —

$$\text{ἅπας δὲ τραχὺς ὅστις ἂν νέον κρατῇ.}$$

Who does not see that the poet, speaking through the mouth of the Fire-god, — who, by the way, is not so very resentful against Prometheus for stealing his attribute of fire, — condemns Zeus as sweeping too clean with his new broom of power?

Upon the whole, I am willing to believe that the last play of the trilogy, if extant, would *modify* the feelings which this drama leaves on the mind. I am willing also to admit, that the sympathy on behalf of Prometheus exacted by the present play is more a modern feeling, than one which would be awakened in the breasts of an Athenian audience. But if they did not go along with the sufferer in their sensibilities, surely they cannot have abstained from compassionating Io, whose wrongs at the hand of Zeus are not to be explained by any *dénouement* in the third part of the trilogy, and must have been inconsistent with the moral standard of the poet himself. Thus we see that he cannot have intended in this drama to exhibit Zeus as a perfect sovereign, having all the right on his side, but rather as a sovereign who found it necessary to resort to severity in order to establish his power, while the question of the right and wrong of the plans of Zeus is entirely put out of sight. The two foes then came together at the last in a compromise. Prometheus, disclosing an important secret, was treated mildly, while he gave in his adherence to the new government. — 1849

ever the occasion allowed of it. The character of Prometheus, again, is better than old Hesiod represents it. Knowing the cost to himself, he seeks to save man from ignorance and ruin. Prometheus has been compared to Milton's Satan, but differs essentially from him as a character of poetry. They are both proud and unyielding; but Satan breathes despair and malignity; Prometheus, hope and kindness to man. Satan is lofty beyond all other characters of poetry, but can draw forth none of that sympathy which moves freely for Prometheus.

Æschylus wrote three or four plays upon the story of Prometheus. One of these, called Prometheus Πυρκαεύς, was a satyric drama, and was acted with Phineus, Persæ, and Glaucus Potnieus, when Meno was archon (Olymp. 67. 4, B. C. 372), as we learn from the argument of Persæ. If this was distinct from the Prometheus Πυρφόρος, we have three tragedies, which may have been exhibited together, relating, according to the practice of Æschylus, like Agamemnon, Choëphori, and the Furies, to the same story. This being admitted, — which a modern scholar of great learning and ingenuity, Professor Welcker, of Bonn, tries to show in his Æschylische Trilogie, — the Πυρφόρος would of course occupy the first place. It must have represented the act of carrying off fire from the smithy of Vulcan on the volcanic mountain Mosychlus, in the island of Lemnos; and may have described the marriage of Prometheus and Hesione. (See v. 555 of the present play.) In the second play we have the penalty of Prometheus: at the end he is covered with fragments of riven rocks, and hidden from sight. After a long time he emerges on Mount Caucasus, where the eagle preys on his liver. Here the scene of the Prometheus *Loosed* is laid, in which the Titans, now released from confinement, form the Chorus. Hercules shoots the eagle with an arrow, and frees Prometheus; while the latter relates to Hercules some of the adventures which he is to meet with. Thus we have in the three dramas, crime, punishment, and reconciliation; and whether exhibited together or not, they form a dramatic whole. Those who wish to enter further into this matter are referred to Welcker's book above mentioned, and to Hermann's dissertation on the other side, " De Æschyli Prometheo Soluto," in his Opuscula, Vol. IV.*

The place where Prometheus is chained, in the present piece, is a rock in European Scythia (2), separated from Mount Caucasus on the west by the country of the Nomad Scythians, by that of the Chalybes, and by the course of the Hybristes, and lying on the sea-coast. (707–719, 422, 573.) The sea in the poet's mind may have been the Hyperborean or Scythian. (See 712, note.) Herein he departed from the received fable, of which the scene was Caucasus, and chose a place where his Chorus of ocean-nymphs could more conveniently assemble. Welcker, however, maintains, with the writers of the argument, that a point of Caucasus below the summit of the mountain was intended to be the scene of the drama: — indeed, he seems to think a difference fatal to the theory that the *Bound* and *Loosed* Prometheus were acted together. But, with Völcker (Mythische Geographie, p. 200), we may say, that Prometheus, after being buried among the rocks (1019), may have emerged on Caucasus. Most of the best scholars who have expressed their opinion on this point are against Welcker; such as Porson, Jacobs, Hermann, Schömann, and the author of the excellent little treatise just cited.

The time when the Chained Prometheus was acted is uncertain. There is a prophecy at v. 367 of an eruption of Mount Ætna, which must allude to one that took place ac-

---

* It is understood that, in a program of the year 1846, Hermann gave up his old position with regard to the Promethean trilogy, and acceded to Welcker's views. — 1849.

cording to the Parian Chronicle in Olymp. 75. 2, or according to Thucydides (3, sub fin.) several years later. This was the second eruption after the settlement of the Greeks in Sicily, and indeed the first of which any thing besides the mere event is known. Again, vv. 347–372 contain, as I think, a clear imitation of Pindar's first Pythian, which was composed Olymp. 77. 3; or, as Boeckh (on Pind. Pyth. 1) shows, 76. 3. Æschylus went to Sicily after 77. 4, and perhaps stayed there until his death, but still brought forward plays upon the Athenian stage. We seem to have, then, the time before which this part of the play cannot have been written; but the passage may have been added on a reacting in Sicily, — a supposition which will account for its episodical character, and for its being given, in the ordinary text, to the wrong person.

The first edition, with a text chiefly following that of W. Dindorf in his "Poetæ Scenici," appeared in 1837; the second, with an unaltered text, but with many new notes, in 1841. I have now in this third edition corrected and added to the notes, and have made the following changes in the text: — in verse 49, $\dot{\epsilon}\pi\alpha\chi\theta\hat{\eta}$ for $\dot{\epsilon}\pi\rho\dot{\alpha}\chi\theta\eta$; 108, $\dot{\epsilon}\nu\dot{\epsilon}\zeta\epsilon\upsilon\gamma\mu\alpha\iota$ for $\dot{\upsilon}\pi\dot{\epsilon}\zeta\epsilon\upsilon\gamma\mu\alpha\iota$, 113, $\dot{\upsilon}\pi\alpha\dot{\iota}\theta\rho\iota\sigma$ for $\dot{\upsilon}\pi\alpha\iota\theta\rho\dot{\iota}\sigma\iota\varsigma$; 340, $\tau\dot{\alpha}~\mu\dot{\epsilon}\nu$ for $\tau\dot{\alpha}~\mu\dot{\epsilon}\nu$; 345, $\epsilon\ddot{\iota}\nu\epsilon\kappa\alpha$ for $\sigma\ddot{\upsilon}\nu\epsilon\kappa\alpha$; 478, $\dot{\epsilon}\varsigma$ for $\epsilon\dot{\iota}\varsigma$; 481, $\pi\rho\dot{\iota}\nu~\gamma'$ for $\pi\rho\dot{\iota}\nu$; 497, $\dot{\sigma}\sigma\phi\hat{\upsilon}\nu$ for $\dot{\sigma}\sigma\phi\dot{\upsilon}\nu$; 540, $\delta\epsilon\rho\kappa\sigma\mu\dot{\epsilon}\nu\alpha$ for $\delta\epsilon\rho\kappa\sigma\mu\dot{\epsilon}\nu\eta$; 586, $\gamma\epsilon\gamma\upsilon\mu\nu\dot{\alpha}\kappa\alpha\sigma\iota\nu$ for $\gamma\epsilon\gamma\upsilon\mu\nu\dot{\alpha}\kappa\alpha\sigma'$; 606, $\mu\hat{\eta}\chi\alpha\rho~\dot{\eta}$ for $\mu\dot{\eta}~\chi\rho\dot{\eta}$; 659, $\mu\dot{\alpha}\theta\eta$ for $\mu\dot{\alpha}\theta\sigma\iota$; 674, $\kappa\epsilon\rho\alpha\sigma\tau\dot{\iota}\varsigma$ for $\kappa\epsilon\rho\dot{\alpha}\sigma\tau\iota\varsigma$; 705, $\sigma\dot{\upsilon}~\tau'$ for $\sigma\dot{\upsilon}~\delta'$; 829, $\gamma\dot{\alpha}\pi\epsilon\delta\alpha$ for $\delta\dot{\alpha}\pi\epsilon\delta\alpha$; 866, $\xi\dot{\upsilon}\nu\epsilon\upsilon\nu\sigma\nu$ for $\sigma\dot{\upsilon}\nu\epsilon\upsilon\nu\sigma\nu$.

ΑΙΣΧΥΛΟΥ
ΠΡΟΜΗΘΕΥΣ ΔΕΣΜΩΤΗΣ.

ΤΑ ΤΟΥ ΔΡΑΜΑΤΟΣ ΠΡΟΣΩΠΑ.

ΚΡΑΤΟΣ ΚΑΙ ΒΙΑ.
ΗΦΑΙΣΤΟΣ.
ΠΡΟΜΗΘΕΥΣ.
ΧΟΡΟΣ ΩΚΕΑΝΙΔΩΝ ΝΥΜΦΩΝ.

ΩΚΕΑΝΟΣ.
ΙΩ Η ΙΝΑΧΟΥ.
ΕΡΜΗΣ.

ΥΠΟΘΕΣΙΣ.

Προμηθέως ἐν Σκυθίᾳ δεδεμένου διὰ τὸ κεκλοφέναι τὸ πῦρ πυνθάνεται Ἰὼ πλανωμένη ὅτι κατ᾽ Αἴγυπτον γενομένη ἐκ τῆς ἐπαφήσεως τοῦ Διὸς τέξεται τὸν Ἔπαφον. Ἑρμῆς δὲ παράγεται ἀπειλῶν αὐτῷ κεραυνωθήσεσθαι, ἐὰν μὴ εἴπῃ τὰ μέλλοντα ἔσεσθαι τῷ Διί. προέλεγε γὰρ ὁ Προμηθεὺς ὡς ἐξωσθήσεται ὁ Ζεὺς τῆς ἀρχῆς ὑπό τινος οἰκείου υἱοῦ. τέλος δὲ βροντῆς γενομένης ἀφανὴς ὁ Προμηθεὺς γίνεται.

Κεῖται δὲ ἡ μυθοποιία ἐν παρεκβάσει παρὰ Σοφοκλεῖ ἐν Κολχίσι, παρὰ δὲ Εὐριπίδῃ ὅλως οὐ κεῖται. ἡ μὲν σκηνὴ τοῦ δράματος ὑπόκειται ἐν Σκυθίᾳ ἐπὶ τὸ Καυκάσιον ὄρος· ὁ δὲ χορὸς συνέστηκεν ἐξ Ὠκεανίδων νυμφῶν. τὸ δὲ κεφάλαιον αὐτοῦ ἐστι Προμηθέως δέσις.

Ἰστέον δὲ ὅτι οὐ κατὰ τὸν κοινὸν λόγον ἐν Καυκάσῳ φησὶ δεδέσθαι τὸν Προμηθέα, ἀλλὰ πρὸς τοῖς Εὐρωπαίοις μέρεσι τοῦ Ὠκεανοῦ, ὡς ἀπὸ τῶν πρὸς τὴν Ἰὼ λεγομένων ἔξεστι συμβαλεῖν.

ΑΛΛΩΣ.

Προμηθέως ἐκ Διὸς κεκλοφότος τὸ πῦρ καὶ δεδωκότος ἀνθρώποις, δι᾽ οὗ τέχνας πάσας ἄνθρωποι εὕροντο, ὀργισθεὶς ὁ Ζεὺς παραδίδωσιν αὐτὸν Κράτει καὶ Βίᾳ, τοῖς αὑτοῦ ὑπηρέταις, καὶ Ἡφαίστῳ, ὡς ἂν ἀγαγόντες πρὸς τὸ Καυκάσιον ὄρος δεσμοῖς σιδηροῖς αὐτὸν ἐκεῖ προσηλώσαιεν. οὗ γενομένου παραγίνονται πᾶσαι αἱ Ὠκεαναῖαι νύμφαι πρὸς παραμυθίαν αὐτοῦ, καὶ αὐτὸς ὁ Ὠκεανὸς, ὃς δὴ καὶ λέγει τῷ Προμηθεῖ, ἵνα ἀπελθὼν πρὸς τὸν Δία δεήσεσι καὶ λιταῖς πείσῃ αὐτὸν ἐκλῦσαι τοῦ δεσμοῦ Προμηθέα. καὶ Προμηθεὺς οὐκ ἐᾷ, τὸ τοῦ Διὸς εἰδὼς ἄκαμπτον καὶ θρασύ. καὶ ἀναχωρήσαντος τοῦ Ὠκεανοῦ παραγίνεται Ἰὼ πλανωμένη, ἡ τοῦ Ἰνάχου, καὶ μανθάνει παρ' αὐτοῦ ἅ τε πέπονθε καὶ ἃ πείσεται, καὶ ὅτι τὶς τῶν αὐτῆς ἀπογόνων λύσει αὐτὸν, ὃς ἦν ὁ Διὸς Ἡρακλῆς, καὶ ὅτι ἐκ τῆς ἐπαφήσεως τοῦ Διὸς τέξει τὸν Ἔπαφον. Θρασυστομοῦντι δὲ Προμηθεῖ κατὰ Διὸς, ὡς ἐκπευεῖται τῆς ἀρχῆς ὑφ' οὗ τέξεται παιδὸς, καὶ ἄλλα βλάσφημα λέγοντι, παραγίνεται Ἑρμῆς, Διὸς πέμψαντος, ἀπειλῶν αὐτῷ κεραυνὸν, εἰ μὴ τὰ μέλλοντα συμβήσεσθαι τῷ Διὶ εἴπῃ· καὶ μὴ βουλόμενον βροντῇ καταρραγεῖσα αὐτὸν ἀφανίζει.

Ἡ μὲν σκηνὴ τοῦ δράματος ὑπόκειται ἐν Σκυθίᾳ ἐπὶ τὸ Καυκάσιον ὄρος, ἡ δὲ ἐπιγραφὴ τούτου *ΠΡΟΜΗΘΕΥΣ ΔΕΣΜΩΤΗΣ.*

ΠΡΟΜΗΘΕΥΣ ΔΕΣΜΩΤΗΣ.

ΚΡΑΤΟΣ.

Χθονὸς μὲν εἰς τηλουρὸν ἥκομεν πέδον,
Σκύθην ἐς οἶμον, ἄβατον εἰς ἐρημίαν.
Ἥφαιστε, σοὶ δὲ χρὴ μέλειν ἐπιστολὰς
ἅς σοι πατὴρ ἐφεῖτο, τόνδε πρὸς πέτραις
ὑψηλοκρήμνοις τὸν λεωργὸν ὀχμάσαι   5
ἀδαμαντίνων δεσμῶν ἐν ἀρρήκτοις πέδαις.
τὸ σὸν γὰρ ἄνθος, παντέχνου πυρὸς σέλας,
θνητοῖσι κλέψας ὤπασεν· τοιᾶσδέ τοι
ἁμαρτίας σφε δεῖ θεοῖς δοῦναι δίκην,
ὡς ἂν διδαχθῇ τὴν Διὸς τυραννίδα   10
στέργειν, φιλανθρώπου δὲ παύεσθαι τρόπου.

ΗΦΑΙΣΤΟΣ.

Κράτος Βία τε, σφῶν μὲν ἐντολὴ Διὸς
ἔχει τέλος δὴ κοὐδὲν ἐμποδὼν ἔτι·
ἐγὼ δ᾽ ἄτολμός εἰμι συγγενῆ θεὸν
δῆσαι βίᾳ φάραγγι πρὸς δυσχειμέρῳ.   15
πάντως δ᾽ ἀνάγκη τῶνδέ μοι τόλμαν σχεθεῖν·
ἐξωριάζειν γὰρ πατρὸς λόγους βαρύ.
τῆς ὀρθοβούλου Θέμιδος αἰπυμῆτα παῖ,
ἄκοντά σ᾽ ἄκων δυσλύτοις χαλκεύμασι
προσπασσαλεύσω τῷδ᾽ ἀπανθρώπῳ πάγῳ,   20
ἵν᾽ οὔτε φωνὴν οὔτε του μορφὴν βροτῶν

1*

ΑΙΣΧΥΛΟΥ

ὄψει, σταθευτὸς δ᾽ ἡλίου φοίβῃ φλογί
χροιᾶς ἀμείψεις ἄνθος· ἀσμένῳ δέ σοι
ἡ ποικιλείμων νὺξ ἀποκρύψει φάος,
πάχνην θ᾽ ἑῴαν ἥλιος σκεδᾷ πάλιν· 25
ἀεὶ δὲ τοῦ παρόντος ἀχθηδὼν κακοῦ
τρύσει σ᾽· ὁ λωφήσων γὰρ οὐ πέφυκέ πω.
τοιαῦτ᾽ ἀπηύρω τοῦ φιλανθρώπου τρόπου.
θεὸς θεῶν γὰρ οὐχ ὑποπτήσσων χόλον
βροτοῖσι τιμὰς ὤπασας πέρα δίκης. 30
ἀνθ᾽ ὧν ἀτερπῆ τήνδε φρουρήσεις πέτραν,
ὀρθοστάδην, ἄϋπνος, οὐ κάμπτων γόνυ·
πολλοὺς δ᾽ ὀδυρμοὺς καὶ γόους ἀνωφελεῖς
φθέγξει· Διὸς γὰρ δυσπαραίτητοι φρένες·
ἅπας δὲ τραχὺς, ὅστις ἂν νέον κρατῇ. 35

ΚΡΑΤΟΣ.

εἶεν, τί μέλλεις καὶ κατοικτίζει μάτην;
τί τὸν θεοῖς ἔχθιστον οὐ στυγεῖς θεὸν,
ὅστις τὸ σὸν θνητοῖσι προὔδωκεν γέρας;

ΗΦΑΙΣΤΟΣ.

τὸ ξυγγενές τοι δεινὸν ἥ θ᾽ ὁμιλία.

ΚΡΑΤΟΣ.

ξύμφημ᾽, ἀνηκουστεῖν δὲ τῶν πατρὸς λόγων 40
οἷόν τε πῶς; οὐ τοῦτο δειμαίνεις πλέον;

ΗΦΑΙΣΤΟΣ.

ἀεί γε δὴ νηλὴς σὺ καὶ θράσους πλέως.

ΚΡΑΤΟΣ.

ἄκος γὰρ οὐδὲν τόνδε θρηνεῖσθαι· σὺ δὲ
τὰ μηδὲν ὠφελοῦντα μὴ πόνει μάτην.

ΠΡΟΜΗΘΕΥΣ ΔΕΣΜΩΤΗΣ.

ΗΦΑΙΣΤΟΣ.
ὦ πολλὰ μισηθεῖσα χειρωναξία.

ΚΡΑΤΟΣ.
τί νιν στυγεῖς; πόνων γὰρ, ὡς ἁπλῷ λόγῳ,
τῶν νῦν παρόντων οὐδὲν αἰτία τέχνη.

ΗΦΑΙΣΤΟΣ.
ἔμπας τὶς αὐτὴν ἄλλος ὤφελεν λαχεῖν.

ΚΡΑΤΟΣ.
ἅπαντ' ἐπαχθῆ πλὴν θεοῖσι κοιρανεῖν.
ἐλεύθερος γὰρ οὔτις ἐστὶ πλὴν Διός.

ΗΦΑΙΣΤΟΣ.
ἔγνωκα, τοῖσδε κοὐδὲν ἀντειπεῖν ἔχω.

ΚΡΑΤΟΣ.
οὔκουν ἐπείξει δεσμὰ τῷδε περιβαλεῖν,
ὡς μή σ' ἐλινύοντα προσδερχθῇ πατήρ;

ΗΦΑΙΣΤΟΣ.
καὶ δὴ πρόχειρα ψάλια δέρκεσθαι πάρα.

ΚΡΑΤΟΣ.
λαβὼν νιν, ἀμφὶ χερσὶν ἐγκρατεῖ σθένει
ῥαιστῆρι θεῖνε, πασσάλευε πρὸς πέτραις.

ΗΦΑΙΣΤΟΣ.
περαίνεται δὴ κοὐ ματᾷ τοὔργον τόδε.

ΚΡΑΤΟΣ.
ἄρασσε μᾶλλον, σφίγγε, μηδαμῇ χάλα.
δεινὸς γὰρ εὑρεῖν κἀξ ἀμηχάνων πόρους.

ΗΦΑΙΣΤΟΣ.
ἄραρεν ἥδε γ' ὠλένη δυσεκλύτως.

ΚΡΑΤΟΣ.
καὶ τήνδε νῦν πόρπασον ἀσφαλῶς, ἵνα

ΑΙΣΧΥΛΟΥ

μάθη σοφιστὴς ὢν Διὸς νωθέστερος.
ΗΦΑΙΣΤΟΣ.
πλὴν τοῦδ' ἂν οὐδεὶς ἐνδίκως μέμψαιτό μοι.
ΚΡΑΤΟΣ.
ἀδαμαντίνου νῦν σφηνὸς αὐθάδη γνάθον
στέρνων διαμπὰξ πασσάλευ' ἐρρωμένως. 65
ΗΦΑΙΣΤΟΣ.
αἰαῖ, Προμηθεῦ, σῶν ὕπερ στένω πόνων.
ΚΡΑΤΟΣ.
σὺ δ' αὖ κατοκνεῖς, τῶν Διός τ' ἐχθρῶν ὕπερ
στένεις; ὅπως μὴ σαυτὸν οἰκτιεῖς ποτέ.
ΗΦΑΙΣΤΟΣ.
ὁρᾷς θέαμα δυσθέατον ὄμμασιν.
ΚΡΑΤΟΣ.
ὁρῶ κυροῦντα τόνδε τῶν ἐπαξίων. 70
ἀλλ' ἀμφὶ πλευραῖς μασχαλιστῆρας βάλε.
ΗΦΑΙΣΤΟΣ.
δρᾶν ταῦτ' ἀνάγκη, μηδὲν ἐγκέλευ' ἄγαν.
ΚΡΑΤΟΣ.
ἦ μὴν κελεύσω, κἀπιθωΰξω γε πρός.
χώρει κάτω, σκέλη δὲ κίρκωσον βίᾳ.
ΗΦΑΙΣΤΟΣ.
καὶ δὴ πέπρακται τοὔργον οὐ μακρῷ πόνῳ. 75
ΚΡΑΤΟΣ.
ἐρρωμένως νῦν θεῖνε διατόρους πέδας·
ὡς οὑπιτιμητής γε τῶν ἔργων βαρύς.
ΗΦΑΙΣΤΟΣ.
ὅμοια μορφῇ γλῶσσά σου γηρύεται·

ΠΡΟΜΗΘΕΥΣ ΔΕΣΜΩΤΗΣ. 9

ΚΡΑΤΟΣ.
σὺ μαλθακίζου, τὴν δ' ἐμὴν αὐθαδίαν
ὀργῆς τε τραχύτητα μὴ 'πίπλησσέ μοι.   80

ΗΦΑΙΣΤΟΣ.
στείχωμεν, ὡς κώλοισιν ἀμφίβληστρ' ἔχει.

ΚΡΑΤΟΣ.
ἐνταῦθα νῦν ὕβριζε, καὶ θεῶν γέρα
συλῶν, ἐφημέροισι προστίθει. τί σοι
οἷοί τε θνητοὶ τῶνδ' ἀπαντλῆσαι πόνων;
ψευδωνύμως σε δαίμονες Προμηθέα   85
καλοῦσιν· αὐτὸν γάρ σε δεῖ προμηθέως,
ὅτῳ τρόπῳ τῆσδ' ἐκκυλισθήσει τέχνης.

ΠΡΟΜΗΘΕΥΣ.
ὦ δῖος αἰθὴρ καὶ ταχύπτεροι πνοαὶ,
ποταμῶν τε πηγαὶ, ποντίων τε κυμάτων
ἀνήριθμον γέλασμα, παμμῆτόρ τε γῆ,   90
καὶ τὸν πανόπτην κύκλον ἡλίου καλῶ·
ἴδεσθέ μ' οἷα πρὸς θεῶν πάσχω θεός.
δέρχθηθ', οἵαις αἰκίαισιν
διακναιόμενος τὸν μυριετῆ
χρόνον ἀθλεύσω.   95
τοιόνδ' ὁ νέος ταγὸς μακάρων
ἐξεῦρ' ἐπ' ἐμοὶ δεσμὸν ἀεικῆ.
φεῦ φεῦ, τὸ παρὸν τό τ' ἐπερχόμενον
πῆμα στενάχω, πῇ ποτε μόχθων
χρὴ τέρματα τῶνδ' ἐπιτεῖλαι.   100
καίτοι τί φημί; πάντα προὐξεπίσταμαι
σκεθρῶς τὰ μέλλοντ', οὐδέ μοι ποταίνιον
πῆμ' οὐδὲν ἥξει. τὴν πεπρωμένην δὲ χρὴ
αἶσαν φέρειν ὡς ῥᾷστα, γιγνώσκονθ', ὅτι

ΑΙΣΧΥΛΟΥ

τὸ τῆς ἀνάγκης ἔστ' ἀδήριτον σθένος. 105
ἀλλ' οὔτε σιγᾶν οὔτε μὴ σιγᾶν τύχας
οἷόν τέ μοι τάσδ' ἐστί. θνητοῖς γὰρ γέρα
πορὼν, ἀνάγκαις ταῖσδ' ἐνέζευγμαι τάλας·
ναρθηκοπλήρωτον δὲ θηρῶμαι πυρὸς
πηγὴν κλοπαίαν, ἣ διδάσκαλος τέχνης 110
πάσης βροτοῖς πέφηνε καὶ μέγας πόρος.
τοιάσδε ποινὰς ἀμπλακημάτων τίνω,
ὑπαίθριος δεσμοῖσι πασσαλευτὸς ὤν.
ἆ ἆ, ἔα ἔα.
τίς ἀχὼ, τίς ὀδμὰ προσέπτα μ' ἀφεγγὴς, 115
θεόσυτος, ἢ βρότειος, ἢ κεκραμένη;
ἵκετο τερμόνιον ἐπὶ πάγον
πόνων ἐμῶν θεωρὸς, ἦ τί δὴ θέλων;
ὁρᾶτε δεσμώτην με δύσποτμον θεὸν,
τὸν Διὸς ἐχθρὸν, τὸν πᾶσι θεοῖς 120
δι' ἀπεχθείας ἐλθόνθ', ὁπόσοι
τὴν Διὸς αὐλὴν εἰσοιχνεῦσιν,
διὰ τὴν λίαν φιλότητα βροτῶν.
φεῦ φεῦ, τί ποτ' αὖ κινάθισμα κλύω
πέλας οἰωνῶν; αἰθὴρ δ' ἐλαφραῖς 125
πτερύγων ῥιπαῖς ὑποσυρίζει.
πᾶν μοι φοβερὸν τὸ προσέρπον.

ΧΟΡΟΣ.

μηδὲν φοβηθῇς· φιλία γὰρ ἥδε τάξις, πτερύγων
θοαῖς ἁμίλλαις, προσέβα τόνδε πάγον, πατρῴας
μόγις παρειποῦσα φρένας. 130
κραιπνοφόροι δέ μ' ἔπεμψαν αὖραι·

128—135. = 144—151.

ΠΡΟΜΗΘΕΥΣ ΔΕΣΜΩΤΗΣ.

κτύπου γὰρ ἀχὼ χάλυβος
διῆξεν ἄντρων μυχὸν, ἐκ δ' ἔπληξέ μου τὰν θεμε-
     ρῶπιν αἰδῶ·
σύθην δ' ἀπέδιλος ὄχῳ πτερωτῷ.   — 135
    ΠΡΟΜΗΘΕΥΣ.

αἰαῖ, αἰαῖ,
τῆς πολυτέκνου Τηθύος ἔκγονα,
τοῦ περὶ πᾶσάν θ' εἱλισσομένου
χθόν' ἀκοιμήτῳ ῥεύματι παῖδες
πατρὸς Ὠκεανοῦ· δέρχθητ', ἐσίδεσθ',   140
οἵῳ δεσμῷ προσπορπατὸς
τῆσδε φάραγγος σκοπέλοις ἐν ἄκροις
φρουρὰν ἄζηλον ὀχήσω.
    ΧΟΡΟΣ.

λεύσσω, Προμηθεῦ· φοβερὰ δ' ἐμοῖσιν ὄσσοις
    ὀμίχλα
προσῇξε πλήρης δακρύων, σὸν δέμας εἰσιδοῦσα 145
πέτραις προσαυαινόμενον
ταῖς ἀδαμαντοδέτοισι λύμαις·
νέοι γὰρ οἰακονόμοι
κρατοῦσ' Ὀλύμπου· νεοχμοῖς δὲ δὴ νόμοις Ζεὺς
    ἀθέτως κρατύνει   150
τὰ πρὶν δὲ πελώρια νῦν ἀϊστοῖ.
    ΠΡΟΜΗΘΕΥΣ.

εἰ γάρ μ' ὑπὸ γῆν νέρθεν τ' Ἀΐδου
τοῦ νεκροδέγμονος εἰς ἀπέραντον
Τάρταρον ἧκεν,
δεσμοῖς ἀλύτοις ἀγρίως πελάσας,   155
ὡς μήτε θεὸς μήτε τις ἄλλος

12 ΑΙΣΧΥΛΟΥ

τοῖσδ' ἐπεγήθει.
νῦν δ' αἰθέριον κίνυγμ' ὁ τάλας
ἐχθροῖς ἐπίχαρτα πέπονθα.

ΧΟΡΟΣ.

τίς ὧδε τλησικάρδιος
θεῶν, ὅτῳ τάδ' ἐπιχαρῇ;   160
τίς οὐ ξυνασχαλᾷ κακοῖς
τεοῖσι, δίχα γε Διός; ὁ δ' ἐπικότως ἀεὶ
τιθέμενος ἄγναμπτον νόον,
δάμναται οὐρανίαν
γένναν· οὐδὲ λήξει, πρὶν ἂν ἢ κορέσῃ κέαρ, ἢ
παλάμᾳ τινὶ   165
τὰν δυσάλωτον ἕλῃ τις ἀρχάν.

ΠΡΟΜΗΘΕΥΣ.

ἦ μὴν ἔτ' ἐμοῦ, καίπερ κρατεραῖς
ἐν γυιοπέδαις αἰκιζομένου,
χρείαν ἕξει μακάρων πρύτανις,
δεῖξαι τὸ νέον βούλευμ' ὑφ' ὅτου   170
σκῆπτρον τιμάς τ' ἀποσυλᾶται.
καί μ' οὔτι μελιγλώσσοις πειθοῦς
ἐπαοιδαῖσιν
θέλξει, στερεάς τ' οὔποτ' ἀπειλὰς
πτήξας τόδ' ἐγὼ καταμηνύσω,   175
πρὶν ἂν ἐξ ἀγρίων δεσμῶν χαλάσῃ,
ποινάς τε τίνειν
τῆσδ' αἰκίας ἐθελήσῃ.

ΧΟΡΟΣ.

σὺ μὲν θρασύς τε καὶ πικραῖς
δύαισιν οὐδὲν ἐπιχαλᾷς,

159 - - 166. = 178 — 185.

ΠΡΟΜΗΘΕΥΣ ΔΕΣΜΩΤΗΣ.

ἄγαν δ' ἐλευθεροστομεῖς. 180
ἐμὰς δὲ φρένας ἐρέθισε διάτορος φόβος
δέδια γὰρ ἀμφὶ σαῖς τύχαις,
πᾶ ποτε τῶνδε πόνων
χρή σε τέρμα κέλσαντ' ἐσιδεῖν. ἀχίχητα γὰρ ἤθεα
    καὶ κέαρ
ἀπαράμυθον ἔχει Κρόνου παῖς. 185

ΠΡΟΜΗΘΕΥΣ.

οἶδ' ὅτι τραχὺς καὶ παρ' ἑαυτῷ
τὸ δίκαιον ἔχων Ζεύς· ἀλλ' ἔμπας
μαλαχογνώμων
ἔσται ποθ', ὅταν ταύτῃ ῥαισθῇ·
τὴν δ' ἀτέραμνον στορέσας ὀργὴν, 190
εἰς ἀρθμὸν ἐμοὶ καὶ φιλότητα
σπεύδων σπεύδοντί ποθ' ἥξει.

ΧΟΡΟΣ.

πάντ' ἐκκάλυψον καὶ γέγων' ἡμῖν λόγον,
ποίῳ λαβών σε Ζεὺς ἐπ' αἰτιάματι,
οὕτως ἀτίμως καὶ πικρῶς αἰκίζεται· 195
δίδαξον ἡμᾶς, εἴ τι μὴ βλάπτει λόγῳ.

ΠΡΟΜΗΘΕΥΣ.

ἀλγεινὰ μέν μοι καὶ λέγειν ἐστὶν τάδε,
ἄλγος δὲ σιγᾶν, πανταχῇ δὲ δύσποτμα.
ἐπεὶ τάχιστ' ἤρξαντο δαίμονες χόλου,
στάσις τ' ἐν ἀλλήλοισιν ὠροθύνετο, — 200
οἱ μὲν θέλοντες ἐκβαλεῖν ἕδρης Κρόνον,
ὡς Ζεὺς ἀνάσσῃ δῆθεν, οἱ δὲ τοὔμπαλιν
σπεύδοντες, ὡς Ζεὺς μήποτ' ἄρξειεν θεῶν, —
ἐνταῦθ' ἐγὼ τὰ λῷστα βουλεύων, πιθεῖν

Τιτᾶνας, Οὐρανοῦ τε καὶ Χθονὸς τέκνα,
οὐκ ἠδυνήθην· αἱμύλας δὲ μηχανὰς
ἀτιμάσαντες καρτεροῖς φρονήμασιν,
ᾤοντ' ἀμοχθὶ πρὸς βίαν τε δεσπόσειν·
ἐμοὶ δὲ μήτηρ οὐχ ἅπαξ μόνον Θέμις,
καὶ Γαῖα πολλῶν ὀνομάτων μορφὴ μία,
τὸ μέλλον ᾗ κραίνοιτο προυτεθεσπίκει,
ὡς οὐ κατ' ἰσχὺν οὐδὲ πρὸς τὸ καρτερὸν
χρείη, δόλῳ δὲ τοὺς ὑπερέχοντας κρατεῖν.
τοιαῦτ' ἐμοῦ λόγοισιν ἐξηγουμένου,
οὐκ ἠξίωσαν οὐδὲ προσβλέψαι τὸ πᾶν.
κράτιστα δή μοι τῶν παρεστώτων τότε
ἐφαίνετ' εἶναι προσλαβόντα μητέρα
ἑκόνθ' ἑκόντι Ζηνὶ συμπαραστατεῖν.
ἐμαῖς δὲ βουλαῖς Ταρτάρου μελαμβαθὴς
κευθμὼν καλύπτει τὸν παλαιγενῆ Κρόνον
αὐτοῖσι συμμάχοισι. τοιάδ' ἐξ ἐμοῦ
ὁ τῶν θεῶν τύραννος ὠφελημένος
κακαῖσι ποιναῖς ταῖσδέ μ' ἐξημείψατο.
ἔνεστι γάρ πως τοῦτο τῇ τυραννίδι
νόσημα, τοῖς φίλοισι μὴ πεποιθέναι.
ὃ δ' οὖν ἐρωτᾶτ', αἰτίαν καθ' ἥντινα
αἰκίζεταί με, τοῦτο δὴ σαφηνιῶ.
ὅπως τάχιστα τὸν πατρῷον ἐς θρόνον
καθέζετ', εὐθὺς δαίμοσιν νέμει γέρα
ἄλλοισιν ἄλλα, καὶ διεστοιχίζετο
ἀρχήν· βροτῶν δὲ τῶν ταλαιπώρων λόγον
οὐκ ἔσχεν οὐδέν', ἀλλ' ἀϊστώσας γένος
τὸ πᾶν ἔχρῃζεν ἄλλο φιτῦσαι νέον.
καὶ τοῖσιν οὐδεὶς ἀντέβαινε πλὴν ἐμοῦ.

ΠΡΟΜΗΘΕΥΣ ΔΕΣΜΩΤΗΣ. 15

ἐγὼ δ' ἐτόλμησ'· ἐξελυσάμην βροτοὺς 235
τοῦ μὴ διαῤῥαισθέντας εἰς Ἅιδου μολεῖν.
τῷ τοι τοιαῖσδε πημοναῖσι κάμπτομαι,
πάσχειν μὲν ἀλγειναῖσιν, οἰκτραῖσιν δ' ἰδεῖν·
θνητοὺς δ' ἐν οἴκτῳ προθέμενος, τούτου τυχεῖν
οὐκ ἠξιώθην αὐτός, ἀλλὰ νηλεῶς 240
ὧδ' ἐῤῥύθμισμαι, Ζηνὶ δυσκλεὴς θέα.

ΧΟΡΟΣ.

σιδηρόφρων τε κἀκ πέτρας εἰργασμένος,
ὅστις, Προμηθεῦ, σοῖσιν οὐ ξυνασχαλᾷ
μόχθοις· ἐγὼ γὰρ οὔτ' ἂν εἰσιδεῖν τάδε
ἔχρῃζον, εἰσιδοῦσά τ' ἠλγύνθην κέαρ. 245

ΠΡΟΜΗΘΕΥΣ.

καὶ μὴν φίλοις ἐλεινὸς εἰσορᾶν ἐγώ.

ΧΟΡΟΣ.

μή πού τι προὔβης τῶνδε καὶ περαιτέρω;

ΠΡΟΜΗΘΕΥΣ.

θνητοὺς γ' ἔπαυσα μὴ προδέρκεσθαι μόρον.

ΧΟΡΟΣ.

τὸ ποῖον εὑρὼν τῆσδε φάρμακον νόσου;

ΠΡΟΜΗΘΕΥΣ.

τυφλὰς ἐν αὐτοῖς ἐλπίδας κατῴκισα. 250

ΧΟΡΟΣ.

μέγ' ὠφέλημα τοῦτ' ἐδωρήσω βροτοῖς.

ΠΡΟΜΗΘΕΥΣ.

πρὸς τοῖσδε μέντοι πῦρ ἐγώ σφιν ὤπασα.

ΧΟΡΟΣ.

καὶ νῦν φλογωπὸν πῦρ ἔχουσ' ἐφήμεροι;

ΑΙΣΧΥΛΟΥ

ΠΡΟΜΗΘΕΥΣ

ἀφ' οὗ γε πολλὰς ἐκμαθήσονται τέχνας.

ΧΟΡΟΣ.

τοιοῖσδε δή σε Ζεὺς ἐπ' αἰτιάμασιν 255
αἰκίζεταί τε κοὐδαμῇ χαλᾷ κακῶν,
οὐδ' ἔστιν ἄθλου τέρμα σοι προκείμενον;

ΠΡΟΜΗΘΕΥΣ.

οὐκ ἄλλο γ' οὐδὲν, πλὴν ὅταν κείνῳ δοκῇ.

ΧΟΡΟΣ.

δόξει δὲ πῶς; τίς ἐλπίς; οὐχ ὁρᾷς ὅτι
ἥμαρτες; ὡς δ' ἥμαρτες, οὔτ' ἐμοὶ λέγειν 260
καθ' ἡδονὴν σοί τ' ἄλγος. ἀλλὰ ταῦτα μὲν
μεθῶμεν, ἄθλων δ' ἔκλυσιν ζήτει τινά.

ΠΡΟΜΗΘΕΥΣ.

ἐλαφρὸν, ὅστις πημάτων ἔξω πόδα
ἔχει, παραινεῖν νουθετεῖν τε τὸν κακῶς
πράσσοντ'· ἐγὼ δὲ ταῦθ' ἅπαντ' ἠπιστάμην. 265
ἑκὼν ἑκὼν ἥμαρτον, οὐκ ἀρνήσομαι·
θνητοῖς δ' ἀρήγων, αὐτὸς εὑρόμην πόνους.
οὐ μήν τι ποιναῖς γ' ᾠόμην τοίαισί με
κατισχνανεῖσθαι πρὸς πέτραις πεδαρσίοις,
τυχόντ' ἐρήμου τοῦδ' ἀγείτονος πάγου. 270
καί μοι τὰ μὲν παρόντα μὴ δύρεσθ' ἄχη,
πεδοῖ δὲ βᾶσαι τὰς προσερπούσας τύχας
ἀκούσαθ', ὡς μάθητε διὰ τέλους τὸ πᾶν.
πείθεσθέ μοι, πείθεσθε, συμπονήσατε
τῷ νῦν μογοῦντι. ταὐτά τοι πλανωμένη 275
πρὸς ἄλλοτ' ἄλλον πημονὴ προσιζάνει.

ΧΟΡΟΣ.

οὐκ ἀκούσαις ἐπεθώϋξας

ΠΡΟΜΗΘΕΥΣ ΔΕΣΜΩΤΗΣ. 17

τοῦτο, Προμηθεῦ.
καὶ νῦν ἐλαφρῷ ποδὶ κραιπνόσυτον
θᾶκον προλιποῦσ', 280
αἰθέρα θ' ἁγνὸν πόρον οἰωνῶν,
ὀκριοέσσῃ χθονὶ τῇδε πελῶ·
τοὺς σοὺς δὲ πόνους
χρῄζω διὰ παντὸς ἀκοῦσαι.

ΩΚΕΑΝΟΣ.

ἥκω δολιχῆς τέρμα κελεύθου,
διαμειψάμενος πρὸς σέ, Προμηθεῦ, 285
τὸν πτερυγωκῆ τόνδ' οἰωνὸν
γνώμῃ στομίων ἄτερ εὐθύνων·
ταῖς σαῖς δὲ τύχαις, ἴσθι, συναλγῶ.
τό τε γάρ με, δοκῶ, ξυγγενὲς οὕτως
ἐσαναγκάζει, 290
χωρίς τε γένους, οὐκ ἔστιν ὅτῳ
μείζονα μοῖραν νείμαιμ' ἢ σοί.
γνώσει δὲ τάδ' ὡς ἔτυμ', οὐδὲ μάτην
χαριτογλωσσεῖν ἔνι μοι· φέρε γὰρ
σήμαιν' ὅ τι χρή σοι ξυμπράσσειν· 295
οὐ γάρ ποτ' ἐρεῖς, ὡς Ὠκεανοῦ
φίλος ἐστὶ βεβαιότερός σοι.

ΠΡΟΜΗΘΕΥΣ.

ἔα, τί χρῆμα; καὶ σὺ δὴ πόνων ἐμῶν
ἥκεις ἐπόπτης; πῶς ἐτόλμησας, λιπὼν
ἐπώνυμόν τε ῥεῦμα καὶ πετρηρεφῆ 300
αὐτόκτιτ' ἄντρα, τὴν σιδηρομήτορα
ἐλθεῖν ἐς αἶαν; ἦ θεωρήσων τύχας
ἐμὰς ἀφῖξαι, καὶ ξυνασχαλῶν κακοῖς;

ΑΙΣΧΥΛΟΥ

δέρχου θέαμα, τόνδε τὸν Διὸς φίλον,
τὸν συγκαταστήσαντα τὴν τυραννίδα, 305
οἴαις ὑπ' αὐτοῦ πημοναῖσι κάμπτομαι.

ΩΚΕΑΝΟΣ.

ὁρῶ, Προμηθεῦ, καὶ παραινέσαι γέ σοι
θέλω τὰ λῷστα, καίπερ ὄντι ποικίλῳ.
γίγνωσκε σαυτὸν, καὶ μεθάρμοσαι τρόπους
νέους· νέος γὰρ καὶ τύραννος ἐν θεοῖς. 310
εἰ δ' ὧδε τραχεῖς καὶ τεθηγμένους λόγους
ῥίψεις, τάχ' ἄν σου, καὶ μακρὰν ἀνωτέρω
θακῶν, κλύοι Ζεὺς, ὥστε σοι τὸν νῦν χόλον
παρόντα μόχθων παιδιὰν εἶναι δοκεῖν.
ἀλλ', ὦ ταλαίπωρ', ἃς ἔχεις ὀργὰς ἄφες, 315
ζήτει δὲ τῶνδε πημάτων ἀπαλλαγάς.
ἀρχαῖ' ἴσως σοι φαίνομαι λέγειν τάδε·
τοιαῦτα μέντοι τῆς ἄγαν ὑψηγόρου
γλώσσης, Προμηθεῦ, τἀπίχειρα γίγνεται.
σὺ δ' οὐδέπω ταπεινὸς, οὐδ' εἴκεις κακοῖς, 320
πρὸς τοῖς παροῦσι δ' ἄλλα προσλαβεῖν θέλεις.
οὔκουν, ἔμοιγε χρώμενος διδασκάλῳ,
πρὸς κέντρα κῶλον ἐκτενεῖς, ὁρῶν ὅτι
τραχὺς μόναρχος οὐδ' ὑπεύθυνος κρατεῖ.
καὶ νῦν ἐγὼ μὲν εἶμι καὶ πειράσομαι, 325
ἐὰν δύνωμαι, τῶνδέ σ' ἐκλῦσαι πόνων·
σὺ δ' ἡσύχαζε, μηδ' ἄγαν λαβροστόμει.
ἢ οὐκ οἶσθ' ἀκριβῶς, ὢν περισσόφρων, ὅτι
γλώσσῃ ματαίᾳ ζημία προστρίβεται;

ΠΡΟΜΗΘΕΥΣ.

ζηλῶ σ' ὁθούνεκ' ἐκτὸς αἰτίας κυρεῖς, 330
πάντων μετασχὼν καὶ τετολμηκὼς ἐμοί.

ΠΡΟΜΗΘΕΥΣ ΔΕΣΜΩΤΗΣ. 19

καὶ νῦν ἔασον, μηδέ σοι μελησάτω.
πάντως γὰρ οὐ πείσεις νιν· οὐ γὰρ εὐπιθής.
πάπταινε δ' αὐτὸς μή τι πημανθῇς ὁδῷ.

ΩΚΕΑΝΟΣ.

πολλῷ γ' ἀμείνων τοὺς πέλας φρενοῦν ἔφυς 335
ἢ σαυτόν· ἔργῳ κοὐ λόγῳ τεκμαίρομαι.
ὁρμώμενον δὲ μηδαμῶς ἀντισπάσῃς·
αὐχῶ γάρ, αὐχῶ τήνδε δωρεὰν ἐμοὶ
δώσειν Δί', ὥστε τῶνδέ σ' ἐκλῦσαι πόνων.

ΠΡΟΜΗΘΕΥΣ.

τὰ μέν σ' ἐπαινῶ, κοὐδαμῇ λήξω ποτέ· 340
προθυμίας γὰρ οὐδὲν ἐλλείπεις. ἀτὰρ
μηδὲν πόνει· μάτην γάρ, οὐδὲν ὠφελῶν
ἐμοί, πονήσεις, εἴ τι καὶ πονεῖν θέλεις.
ἀλλ' ἡσύχαζε, σαυτὸν ἐκποδὼν ἔχων·
ἐγὼ γὰρ οὐκ, εἰ δυστυχῶ, τοῦδ' εἵνεκα 345
θέλοιμ' ἂν ὡς πλείστοισι πημονὰς τυχεῖν.
οὐ δῆτ', ἐπεί με καὶ κασιγνήτου τύχαι
τείρουσ' Ἄτλαντος, ὃς πρὸς ἑσπέρους τόπους
ἕστηκε, κίον' οὐρανοῦ τε καὶ χθονὸς
ὤμοις ἐρείδων, ἄχθος οὐκ εὐάγκαλον. 350
τὸν γηγενῆ τε Κιλικίων οἰκήτορα
ἄντρων ἰδὼν ᾤκτειρα, δάϊον τέρας,
ἑκατογκάρηνον πρὸς βίαν χειρούμενον
Τυφῶνα θοῦρον, πᾶσιν ὃς ἀνέστη θεοῖς,
σμερδναῖσι γαμφηλαῖσι συρίζων φόνον· 355
ἐξ ὀμμάτων δ' ἤστραπτε γοργωπὸν σέλας,
ὡς τὴν Διὸς τυραννίδ' ἐκπέρσων βίᾳ.

ΑΙΣΧΥΛΟΥ

ἀλλ' ἦλθεν αὐτῷ Ζηνὸς ἄγρυπνον βέλος,
καταιβάτης κεραυνὸς ἐκπνέων φλόγα,
ὃς αὐτὸν ἐξέπληξε τῶν ὑψηγόρων   360
κομπασμάτων. φρένας γὰρ εἰς αὐτὰς τυπεὶς
ἐφεψαλώθη κἀξεβροντήθη σθένος.
καὶ νῦν, ἀχρεῖον καὶ παρήορον δέμας,
κεῖται στενωποῦ πλησίον θαλασσίου,
ἰπούμενος ῥίζαισιν Αἰτναίαις ὕπο·   365
κορυφαῖς δ' ἐν ἄκραις ἥμενος μυδροκτυπεῖ
Ἥφαιστος, ἔνθεν ἐκραγήσονταί ποτε
ποταμοὶ πυρὸς δάπτοντες ἀγρίαις γνάθοις
τῆς καλλικάρπου Σικελίας λευροὺς γύας·
τοιόνδε Τυφὼς ἐξαναζέσει χόλον   370
θερμοῖς ἀπλήστου βέλεσι πυρπνόου ζάλης,
καίπερ κεραυνῷ Ζηνὸς ἠνθρακωμένος.
σὺ δ' οὐκ ἄπειρος, οὐδ' ἐμοῦ διδασκάλου
χρῄζεις· σεαυτὸν σῷζ' ὅπως ἐπίστασαι·
ἐγὼ δὲ τὴν παροῦσαν ἀντλήσω τύχην,   375
ἔς τ' ἂν Διὸς φρόνημα λωφήσῃ χόλου.
    ΩΚΕΑΝΟΣ.
οὔκουν, Προμηθεῦ, τοῦτο γιγνώσκεις, ὅτι
ὀργῆς νοσούσης εἰσὶν ἰατροὶ λόγοι;
    ΠΡΟΜΗΘΕΥΣ.
ἐάν τις ἐν καιρῷ γε μαλθάσσῃ κέαρ,
καὶ μὴ σφριγῶντα θυμὸν ἰσχναίνῃ βίᾳ.   380
    ΩΚΕΑΝΟΣ.
ἐν τῷ προθυμεῖσθαι δὲ καὶ τολμᾶν τίνα
ὁρᾷς ἐνοῦσαν ζημίαν; δίδασκέ με.

ΠΡΟΜΗΘΕΥΣ ΔΕΣΜΩΤΗΣ. 21

ΠΡΟΜΗΘΕΥΣ.
μόχθον περισσὸν, κουφόνουν τ' εὐηθίαι

ΩΚΕΑΝΟΣ.
ἔα με τῇδε τῇ νόσῳ νοσεῖν, ἐπεὶ
κέρδιστον εὖ φρονοῦντα μὴ δοκεῖν φρονεῖν.   385

ΠΡΟΜΗΘΕΥΣ.
ἐμὸν δοκήσει τἀμπλάκημ' εἶναι τόδε.

ΩΚΕΑΝΟΣ.
σαφῶς μ' ἐς οἶκον σὸς λόγος στέλλει πάλιν.

ΠΡΟΜΗΘΕΥΣ.
μὴ γάρ σε θρῆνος οὑμὸς εἰς ἔχθραν βάλῃ.

ΩΚΕΑΝΟΣ.
ἦ τῷ νέον θακοῦντι παγκρατεῖς ἕδρας;

ΠΡΟΜΗΘΕΥΣ.†
τούτου φυλάσσου μή ποτ' ἀχθεσθῇ κέαρ.   390

ΩΚΕΑΝΟΣ.
ἡ σή, Προμηθεῦ, ξυμφορὰ διδάσκαλος.

ΠΡΟΜΗΘΕΥΣ.
στέλλου, κομίζου, σῷζε τὸν παρόντα νοῦν.

ΩΚΕΑΝΟΣ.
ὁρμωμένῳ μοι τόνδ' ἐθώϋξας λόγον.
λευρὸν γὰρ οἶμον αἰθέρος ψαίρει πτεροῖς
τετρασκελὴς οἰωνός· ἄσμενος δέ τἂν   395
σταθμοῖς ἐν οἰκείοισι κάμψειεν γόνυ.

ΧΟΡΟΣ.
στένω σε τᾶς οὐλομένας τύχας, Προμηθεῦ,
δακρυσίστακτον δ' ἀπ' ὄσσων ῥαδινῶν λειβομένα
ῥέος, παρειὰν   400
νοτίοις ἔτεγξα παγαῖς· ἀμέγαρτα γὰρ τάδε Ζεὺς
397 — 405. = 406 — 414.

ἰδίοις νόμοις κρατύνων, ὑπερήφανον θεοῖς τοῖς
πάρος ἐνδείκνυσιν αἰχμάν. 405
πρόπασα δ' ἤδη στονόεν λέλακε χώρα,
μεγαλοσχήμονά τ' ἀρχαιοπρεπῆ *στένουσα τὰν σὰν
ξυνομαιμόνων τε τιμὰν, ὁπόσοι τ' ἔποικον ἁγνᾶς 410
Ἀσίας ἕδος νέμονται, μεγαλοστόνοισι σοῖς πή-
μασι συγκάμνουσι θνητοί·
Κολχίδος τε γᾶς ἔνοικοι 415
παρθένοι, μάχας ἄτρεστοι,
καὶ Σκύθης ὅμιλος, οἳ γᾶς
ἔσχατον τόπον ἀμφὶ Μαιῶτιν ἔχουσι λίμναν,
Ἀραβίας τ' ἄρειον ἄνθος, 420
ὑψίκρημνόν θ' οἳ πόλισμα
Καυκάσου πέλας νέμονται,
δάϊος στρατὸς, ὀξυπρώροισι βρέμων ἐν αἰχμαῖς.
μόνον δὴ πρόσθεν ἄλλον ἐν πόνοις 425
δαμέντ' ἀδαμαντοδέτοις Τιτᾶνα λύμαις
εἰσιδόμαν θεὸν Ἄτλαν,
ὃς αἰὲν ὑπέροχον σθένος κραταιὸν
οὐράνιόν τε πόλον νώτοις ὑποστενάζει. 430
βοᾷ δὲ πόντιος κλύδων
ξυμπιτνῶν, στένει βυθὸς,
κελαινὸς Ἄϊδος δ' ὑποβρέμει μυχὸς γᾶς,
παγαί θ' ἁγνορύτων ποταμῶν στένουσιν ἄλγος
οἰκτρόν. 435

ΠΡΟΜΗΘΕΥΣ.
μή τοι χλιδῇ δοκεῖτε μηδ' αὐθαδίᾳ
σιγᾶν με· συννοίᾳ δὲ δάπτομαι κέαρ,
ὁρῶν ἐμαυτὸν ὧδε προυσελούμενον

415 — 419. = 420 — 424.

καίτοι θεοῖσι τοῖς νέοις τούτοις γέρα
τίς ἄλλος ἢ 'γὼ παντελῶς διώρισεν ; 440
ἀλλ' αὐτὰ σιγῶ. καὶ γὰρ εἰδυίαισιν ἂν
ὑμῖν λέγοιμι· τἀν βροτοῖς δὲ πήματα
ἀκούσαθ', ὡς σφᾶς, νηπίους ὄντας τὸ πρὶν,
ἔννους ἔθηκα καὶ φρενῶν ἐπηβόλους,—
λέξω δὲ, μέμψιν οὔτιν' ἀνθρώποις ἔχων, 445
ἀλλ' ὧν δέδωκ' εὔνοιαν ἐξηγούμενος,—
οἳ πρῶτα μὲν βλέποντες ἔβλεπον μάτην,
κλύοντες οὐκ ἤκουον, ἀλλ' ὀνειράτων
ἀλίγκιοι μορφαῖσι τὸν μακρὸν χρόνον
ἔφυρον εἰκῇ πάντα, κοὔτε πλινθυφεῖς 450
δόμους προσείλους ᾖσαν, οὐ ξυλουργίαν·
κατώρυχες δ' ἔναιον, ὥστ' ἀήσυροι
μύρμηκες, ἄντρων ἐν μυχοῖς ἀνηλίοις.
ἦν δ' οὐδὲν αὐτοῖς οὔτε χείματος τέκμαρ
οὔτ' ἀνθεμώδους ἦρος οὔτε καρπίμου 455
θέρους βέβαιον, ἀλλ' ἄτερ γνώμης τὸ πᾶν
ἔπρασσον, ἔς τε δή σφιν ἀντολὰς ἐγὼ
ἄστρων ἔδειξα τάς τε δυσκρίτους δύσεις.
καὶ μὴν ἀριθμὸν, ἔξοχον σοφισμάτων,
ἐξεῦρον αὐτοῖς, γραμμάτων τε συνθέσεις, 460
μνήμην θ' ἁπάντων μουσομήτορ' ἐργάτιν.
κἄζευξα πρῶτος ἐν ζυγοῖσι κνώδαλα
ζεύγλαισι δουλεύοντα· σώμασίν θ' ὅπως
θνητοῖς μεγίστων διάδοχοι μοχθημάτων
γένωνθ', ὑφ' ἅρματ' ἤγαγον φιληνίους 465
ἵππους, ἄγαλμα τῆς ὑπερπλούτου χλιδῆς.
θαλασσόπλαγκτα δ' οὔτις ἄλλος ἀντ' ἐμοῦ
λινόπτερ' εὗρε ναυτίλων ὀχήματα.

τοιαυτα μηχανήματ' ἐξευρὼν τάλας
βροτοῖσιν, αὐτὸς οὐκ ἔχω σόφισμ', ὅτῳ
τῆς νῦν παρούσης πημονῆς ἀπαλλαγῶ.
ΧΟΡΟΣ.
πέπονθας αἰκὲς πῆμ'· ἀποσφαλεὶς φρενῶν
πλανᾷ· κακὸς δ' ἰατρὸς ὥς τις ἐς νόσον
πεσὼν ἀθυμεῖς, καὶ σεαυτὸν οὐκ ἔχεις
εὑρεῖν ὁποίοις φαρμάκοις ἰάσιμος.
ΠΡΟΜΗΘΕΥΣ.
τὰ λοιπά μου κλύουσα θαυμάσει πλέον,
οἵας τέχνας τε καὶ πόρους ἐμησάμην.
τὸ μὲν μέγιστον, εἴ τις ἐς νόσον πέσοι,
οὐκ ἦν ἀλέξημ' οὐδὲν οὔτε βρώσιμον,
οὐ χριστὸν, οὔτε πιστὸν, ἀλλὰ φαρμάκων
χρείᾳ κατεσκέλλοντο, πρίν γ' ἐγὼ σφίσιν
ἔδειξα κράσεις ἠπίων ἀκεσμάτων,
αἷς τὰς ἁπάσας ἐξαμύνονται νόσους.
τρόπους δὲ πολλοὺς μαντικῆς ἐστοίχισα,
κἄκρινα πρῶτος ἐξ ὀνειράτων ἃ χρὴ
ὕπαρ γενέσθαι, κληδόνας τε δυσκρίτους
ἐγνώρισ' αὐτοῖς· ἐνοδίους τε συμβόλους
γαμψωνύχων τε πτῆσιν οἰωνῶν σκεθρῶς
διώρισ', οἵτινές τε δεξιοὶ φύσιν
εὐωνύμους τε, καὶ δίαιταν ἥντινα
ἔχουσ' ἕκαστοι, καὶ πρὸς ἀλλήλους τίνες
ἔχθραι τε καὶ στέργηθρα καὶ συνεδρίαι·
σπλάγχνων τε λειότητα, καὶ χροιὰν τίνα
ἔχοντ' ἂν εἴη δαίμοσιν πρὸς ἡδονὴν,
χολῆς λοβοῦ τε ποικίλην εὐμορφίαν,

κνίσῃ τε κῶλα συγκαλυπτά· καὶ μακρὰν
ὀσφῦν πυρώσας, δυστέκμαρτον εἰς τέχνην
ὥδωσα θνητούς· καὶ φλογωπὰ σήματα
ἐξωμμάτωσα, πρόσθεν ὄντ' ἐπάργεμα.
τοιαῦτα μὲν δὴ ταῦτ'· ἔνερθε δὲ χθονὸς   500
κεκρυμμέν' ἀνθρώποισιν ὠφελήματα,
χαλκὸν, σίδηρον, ἄργυρον, χρυσόν τε τίς
φήσειεν ἂν πάροιθεν ἐξευρεῖν ἐμοῦ;
οὐδεὶς, σάφ' οἶδα, μὴ μάτην φλῦσαι θέλων.
βραχεῖ δὲ μύθῳ πάντα συλλήβδην μάθε,   505
πᾶσαι τέχναι βροτοῖσιν ἐκ Προμηθέως.

ΧΟΡΟΣ.
μή νυν βροτοὺς μὲν ὠφέλει καιροῦ πέρα,
σαυτοῦ δ' ἀκήδει δυστυχοῦντος· ὡς ἐγὼ
εὔελπίς εἰμι τῶνδέ σ' ἐκ δεσμῶν ἔτι
λυθέντα μηδὲν μεῖον ἰσχύσειν Διός.   510

ΠΡΟΜΗΘΕΥΣ.
οὐ ταῦτα ταύτῃ μοῖρά πω τελεσφόρος
κρᾶναι πέπρωται, μυρίαις δὲ πημοναῖς
δύαις τε καμφθεὶς, ὧδε δεσμὰ φυγγάνω·
τέχνη δ' ἀνάγκης ἀσθενεστέρα μακρῷ.

ΧΟΡΟΣ.
τίς οὖν ἀνάγκης ἐστὶν οἰακοστρόφος;   515

ΠΡΟΜΗΘΕΥΣ.
μοῖραι τρίμορφοι, μνήμονές τ' Ἐρινύες.

ΧΟΡΟΣ.
τούτων ἄρα Ζεύς ἐστιν ἀσθενέστερος.

ΠΡΟΜΗΘΕΥΣ.
οὔκουν ἂν ἐκφύγοι γε τὴν πεπρωμένην.

ΧΟΡΟΣ.
τί γὰρ πέπρωται Ζηνὶ, πλὴν ἀεὶ κρατεῖν;
ΠΡΟΜΗΘΕΥΣ.
τοῦτ' οὐκ ἔτ' ἂν πύθοιο, μηδὲ λιπάρει.   520
ΧΟΡΟΣ.
ἦ πού τι σεμνόν ἐστιν ὃ ξυναμπέχεις.
ΠΡΟΜΗΘΕΥΣ.
ἄλλου λόγου μέμνησθε, τόνδε δ' οὐδαμῶς
καιρὸς γεγωνεῖν, ἀλλὰ συγκαλυπτέος
ὅσον μάλιστα· τόνδε γὰρ σώζων, ἐγὼ
δεσμοὺς ἀεικεῖς καὶ δύας ἐκφυγγάνω.   525
ΧΟΡΟΣ.
μηδάμ' ὁ πάντα νέμων
θεῖτ' ἐμᾷ γνώμᾳ κράτος ἀντίπαλον Ζεὺς,
μηδ' ἐλινύσαιμι θεοὺς ὁσίαις θοίναις ποτινισ-
      σομένα   530
βουφόνοις, παρ' Ὠκεανοῦ πατρὸς ἄσβεστον πόρον,
μηδ' ἀλίτοιμι λόγοις·
ἀλλά μοι τόδ' ἐμμένοι,
καὶ μήποτ' ἐκτακείη.   535
ἡδύ τι θαρσαλέαις
τὸν μακρὸν τείνειν βίον ἐλπίσι, φαναῖς
θυμὸν ἀλδαίνουσαν ἐν εὐφροσύναις. φρίσσω δέ σε
      δερκομένα   540
μυρίοις μόχθοις διακναιόμενον * * *.
Ζῆνα γὰρ οὐ τρομέων,
ἰδίᾳ γνώμῃ σέβει
θνατοὺς ἄγαν, Προμηθεῦ.
      526 — 535. = 536 — 544.

φέρ' ὅπως ἄχαρις χάρις, ὦ φίλος, εἰπὲ, ποῦ τίς
                                    ἀλκά;   545
τίς ἐφαμερίων ἄρηξις; οὐδ' ἐδέρχθης
ὀλιγοδρανίαν ἄκικυν,
ἰσόνειρον, ᾇ τὸ φωτῶν
ἀλαὸν * * * γένος ἐμπεποδισμένον;   550
οὔποτε τὰν Διὸς ἁρμονίαν θνατῶν παρεξίασι
                                    βουλαί.
ἔμαθον τάδε, σὰς προσιδοῦσ' ὀλοὰς τύχας, Προ-
                                    μηθεῦ·
τὸ διαμφίδιον δέ μοι μέλος προσέπτα   555
τόδ', ἐκεῖνό θ' ὅτ' ἀμφὶ λουτρὰ
καὶ λέχος σὸν ὑμεναίουν
ἰότατι γάμων, ὅτε τὰν ὁμοπάτριον
ἕδνοις ἄγαγες Ἡσιόναν πιθὼν δάμαρτα κοινό-
                                    λεκτρον.   560

ΙΩ.

τίς γῆ; τί γένος; τίνα φῶ λεύσσειν
τόνδε χαλινοῖς ἐν πετρίνοισιν
χειμαζόμενον;
τίνος ἀμπλακίης ποινὰς ὀλέκει;
σήμηνον ὅπη
γῆς ἡ μογερὰ πεπλάνημαι.   565
ἆ ἆ, ἔα ἔα·
χρίει τις αὖ με τὰν τάλαιναν οἶστρος,
εἴδωλον Ἄργου γηγενοῦς, ἄλευ δᾶ,
[φοβοῦμαι] τὸν μυριωπὸν εἰσορῶσα βούταν.
ὁ δὲ πορεύεται δόλιον ὄμμ' ἔχων,   570
ὃν οὐδὲ κατθανόντα γαῖα κεύθει.

545 — 552. = 553 — 560.

ἀλλά με τὰν τάλαιναν
ἐξ ἐνέρων περῶν κυνηγετεῖ,
πλανᾷ τε νῆστιν ἀνὰ τὰν παραλίαν ψάμμον.
ὑπὸ δὲ κηρόπλαστος ὀτοβεῖ δόναξ
ἀχέτας ὑπνοδόταν νόμον· ἰὼ ἰὼ, πόποι,   575
πυῖ, πόποι, ποῖ μ' ἄγουσι τηλέπλανοι πλάναι.
τί ποτέ μ', ὦ Κρόνιε
παῖ, τί ποτε ταῖσδ' ἐνέζευξας εὑρὼν ἁμαρτοῦσαν ἐν πημοναῖσιν,
ἒ ἒ, οἰστρηλάτῳ δὲ δείματι δειλαίαν   580
παράκοπον ὧδε τείρεις;
πυρί με φλέξον, ἢ χθονὶ κάλυψον, ἢ
ποντίοις δάκεσι δὸς βορὰν,
μηδέ μοι φθονήσῃς
εὐγμάτων, ἄναξ.
ἄδην με πολύπλανοι πλάναι   585
γεγυμνάκασιν, οὐδ' ἔχω μαθεῖν ὅπῃ
πημονὰς ἀλύξω.
κλύεις φθέγμα τᾶς βούκερω παρθένου;

ΠΡΟΜΗΘΕΥΣ.

πῶς δ' οὐ κλύω τῆς οἰστροδινήτου κόρης
τῆς Ἰναχείης; ἢ Διὸς θάλπει κέαρ   590
ἔρωτι, καὶ νῦν τοὺς ὑπερμήκεις δρόμους
Ἥρᾳ στυγητὸς πρὸς βίαν γυμνάζεται.

ΙΩ.

πόθεν ἐμοῦ σὺ πατρὸς ὄνομ' ἀπύεις,
εἰπέ μοι τᾷ μογερᾷ, τίς ὤν, τίς ἄρα μ', ὦ τάλας,
τὰν ταλαίπωρον ὧδ' ἐτήτυμα προσθροεῖς,   595
θεόσυτόν τε νόσον

574—588. = 593—608.

ὠνόμασας, ἃ μαραίνει με χρί-
ουσα κέντροισι φοιταλέοισιν.
ἒ ἔ. σκιρτημάτων δὲ νήστισιν αἰκίαις 600
λαβρόσυτος ἦλθον, Ἥρας
ἐπικότοισι μήδεσι δαμεῖσα. δυσ-
δαιμόνων δὲ τίνες, οἶ, ἒ ἔ,
οἷ᾽ ἐγώ, μογοῦσιν;
ἀλλά μοι τορῶς
τέκμηρον, ὅ τι μ᾽ ἐπαμμένει 605
παθεῖν, τί μῆχαρ ἢ τί φάρμακον νόσου
δεῖξον, εἴπερ οἶσθα·
θρόει, φράζε τᾷ δυσπλάνῳ παρθένῳ.

ΠΡΟΜΗΘΕΥΣ.

λέξω τορῶς σοι πᾶν ὅπερ χρῄζεις μαθεῖν,
οὐκ ἐμπλέκων αἰνίγματ᾽, ἀλλ᾽ ἁπλῷ λόγῳ, 610
ὥσπερ δίκαιον πρὸς φίλους οἴγειν στόμα.
πυρὸς βροτοῖς δοτῆρ᾽ ὁρᾷς Προμηθέα.

ΙΩ.

ὦ κοινὸν ὠφέλημα θνητοῖσιν φανείς,
τλῆμον Προμηθεῦ, τοῦ δίκην πάσχεις τάδε;

ΠΡΟΜΗΘΕΥΣ.

ἁρμοῖ πέπαυμαι τοὺς ἐμοὺς θρηνῶν πόνους. 615

ΙΩ.

οὔκουν πόροις ἂν τήνδε δωρεὰν ἐμοί;

ΠΡΟΜΗΘΕΥΣ.

λέγ᾽ ἥντιν᾽ αἰτεῖ· πᾶν γὰρ ἂν πύθοιό μου.

ΙΩ.

σήμηνον ὅστις ἐν φάραγγί σ᾽ ὤχμασε.

ΑΙΣΧΥΛΟΥ

ΠΡΟΜΗΘΕΥΣ.
βούλευμα μὲν τὸ δῖον, Ἡφαίστου δὲ χείρ.
ΙΩ.
ποινὰς δὲ ποίων ἀμπλακημάτων τίνεις;
ΠΡΟΜΗΘΕΥΣ.
τοσοῦτον ἀρκῶ σοι σαφηνίσαι μόνον.
ΙΩ.
καὶ πρός γε τούτοις τέρμα τῆς ἐμῆς πλάνης
δεῖξον τίς ἔσται τῇ ταλαιπώρῳ χρόνος.
ΠΡΟΜΗΘΕΥΣ.
τὸ μὴ μαθεῖν σοι κρεῖσσον ἢ μαθεῖν τάδε.
ΙΩ.
μήτοι με κρύψῃς τοῦθ᾽ ὅπερ μέλλω παθεῖν.
ΠΡΟΜΗΘΕΥΣ.
ἀλλ᾽ οὐ μεγαίρω τοῦδέ σοι δωρήματος.
ΙΩ.
τί δῆτα μέλλεις μὴ οὐ γεγωνίσκειν τὸ πᾶν;
ΠΡΟΜΗΘΕΥΣ.
φθόνος μὲν οὐδεὶς, σὰς δ᾽ ὀκνῶ θρᾶξαι φρένας.
ΙΩ.
μή μου προκήδου μᾶσσον ὡς ἐμοὶ γλυκύ.
ΠΡΟΜΗΘΕΥΣ.
ἐπεὶ προθυμεῖ, χρὴ λέγειν· ἄκουε δή.
ΧΟΡΟΣ.
μήπω γε· μοῖραν δ᾽ ἡδονῆς κἀμοὶ πόρε.
τὴν τῆσδε πρῶτον ἱστορήσωμεν νόσον,
αὐτῆς λεγούσης τὰς πολυφθόρους τύχας·
τὰ λοιπὰ δ᾽ ἄθλων σοῦ διδαχθήτω πάρα.

ΠΡΟΜΗΘΕΥΣ ΔΕΣΜΩΤΗΣ. 31

ΠΡΟΜΗΘΕΥΣ.

σὸν ἔργον, Ἰοῖ, ταῖσδ' ὑπουργῆσαι χάριν, 635
ἄλλως τε πάντως καὶ κασιγνήταις πατρός.
ὡς τἀποκλαῦσαι κἀποδύρασθαι τύχας
ἐνταῦθ', ὅπῃ μέλλει τις οἴσεσθαι δάκρυ
πρὸς τῶν κλυόντων, ἀξίαν τριβὴν ἔχει.

ΙΩ.

οὐκ οἶδ' ὅπως ὑμῖν ἀπιστῆσαί με χρὴ, 640
σαφεῖ δὲ μύθῳ πᾶν ὅπερ προσχρῄζετε
πεύσεσθε· καίτοι καὶ λέγουσ' ὀδύρομαι
θεόσσυτον χειμῶνα καὶ διαφθορὰν
μορφῆς, ὅθεν μοι σχετλίᾳ προσέπτατο.
ἀεὶ γὰρ ὄψεις ἔννυχοι πωλεύμεναι 645
ἐς παρθενῶνας τοὺς ἐμοὺς, παρηγόρουν
λείοισι μύθοις· ὦ μέγ' εὔδαιμον κόρη,
τί παρθενεύει δαρὸν, ἐξόν σοι γάμου
τυχεῖν μεγίστου; Ζεὺς γὰρ ἱμέρου βέλει
πρὸς σοῦ τέθαλπται, καὶ ξυναίρεσθαι Κύπριν 650
θέλει· σὺ δ', ὦ παῖ, μὴ 'πολακτίσῃς λέχος
τὸ Ζηνὸς, ἀλλ' ἔξελθε πρὸς Λέρνης βαθὺν
λειμῶνα, ποίμνας βουστάσεις τε πρὸς πατρὸς,
ὡς ἂν τὸ δῖον ὄμμα λωφήσῃ πόθου.
τοιοῖσδε πάσας εὐφρόνας ὀνείρασι 655
ξυνειχόμην δύστηνος, ἔς τε δὴ πατρὶ
ἔτλην γεγωνεῖν νυκτίφοιτ' ὀνείρατα.
ὁ δ' ἔς τε Πυθὼ κἀπὶ Δωδώνης πυκνοὺς
θεοπρόπους ἴαλλεν, ὡς μάθῃ, τί χρὴ
δρῶντ' ἢ λέγοντα δαίμοσιν πράσσειν φίλα. 660
ἧκον δ' ἀναγγέλλοντες αἰολοστόμους

χρησμοὺς ἀσήμους δυσκρίτως τ' εἰρημένους.
τέλος δ' ἐναργὴς βάξις ἦλθεν, Ἰνάχῳ
σαφῶς ἐπισκήπτουσα καὶ μυθουμένη
ἔξω δόμων τε καὶ πάτρας ὠθεῖν ἐμέ, 665
ἄφετον ἀλᾶσθαι γῆς ἐπ' ἐσχάτοις ὅροις·
κεἰ μὴ θέλοι, πυρωπὸν ἐκ Διὸς μολεῖν
κεραυνὸν, ὃς πᾶν ἐξαϊστώσει γένος.
τοιοῖσδε πεισθεὶς Λοξίου μαντεύμασιν,
ἐξήλασέν με κἀπέκλεισε δωμάτων 670
ἄκουσαν ἄκων· ἀλλ' ἐπηνάγκαζέ νιν
Διὸς χαλινὸς πρὸς βίαν πράσσειν τάδε.
εὐθὺς δὲ μορφὴ καὶ φρένες διάστροφοι
ἦσαν, κεραστὶς δ'., ὡς ὁρᾶτ', ὀξυστόμῳ
μύωπι χρισθεῖσ', ἐμμανεῖ σκιρτήματι 675
ᾖσσον πρὸς εὔποτόν τε Κερχνείας ῥέος
Λέρνης ἄκρην τε· βουκόλος δὲ γηγενὴς
ἄκρατος ὀργὴν Ἄργος ὡμάρτει, πυκνοῖς
ὄσσοις δεδορκὼς τοὺς ἐμοὺς κατὰ στίβους.
ἀπροσδόκητος δ' αὐτὸν αἰφνίδιος μόρος 680
τοῦ ζῆν ἀπεστέρησεν. οἰστρόπληξ δ' ἐγὼ
μάστιγι θείᾳ γῆν πρὸ γῆς ἐλαύνομαι.
κλύεις τὰ πραχθέντ'· εἰ δ' ἔχεις εἰπεῖν ὅ τι
λοιπὸν πόνων, σήμαινε· μηδέ μ' οἰκτίσας
ξύνθαλπε μύθοις ψευδέσιν· νόσημα γὰρ 685
αἴσχιστον εἶναί φημι συνθέτους λόγους.

ΧΟΡΟΣ.

ἔα ἔα, ἄπεχε, φεῦ·
οὔποτ' οὔποτ' ηὔχουν ξένους μολεῖσθαι λόγους
ἐς ἀκοὰν ἐμάν, 690

οὐδ' ὧδε δυσθέατα καὶ δύσοιστα
πήματα, λύματα, δείματ' ἀμφήκει
κέντρῳ ψύχειν ψυχὰν ἐμάν·
ἰὼ ἰὼ μοῖρα μοῖρα,
πέφρικ' εἰσιδοῦσα πρᾶξιν Ἰοῦς. 695

ΠΡΟΜΗΘΕΥΣ.
πρό γε στενάζεις καὶ φόβου πλέα τις εἶ·
ἐπίσχες ἔς τ' ἂν καὶ τὰ λοιπὰ προσμάθῃς.

ΧΟΡΟΣ.
λέγ', ἐκδίδασκε· τοῖς νοσοῦσί τοι γλυκὺ
τὸ λοιπὸν ἄλγος προὐξεπίστασθαι τορῶς.

ΠΡΟΜΗΘΕΥΣ.
τὴν πρίν γε χρείαν ἠνύσασθ' ἐμοῦ πάρα 700
κούφως· μαθεῖν γὰρ τῆσδε πρῶτ' ἐχρῄζετε
τὸν ἀμφ' ἑαυτῆς ἆθλον ἐξηγουμένης·
τὰ λοιπὰ νῦν ἀκούσαθ', οἷα χρὴ πάθη
τλῆναι πρὸς Ἥρας τήνδε τὴν νεάνιδα.
σύ τ', Ἰνάχειον σπέρμα, τοὺς ἐμοὺς λόγους 705
θυμῷ βάλ', ὡς ἂν τέρματ' ἐκμάθῃς ὁδοῦ.
πρῶτον μὲν ἐνθένδ' ἡλίου πρὸς ἀντολὰς
στρέψασα σαυτὴν στεῖχ' ἀνηρότους γύας·
Σκύθας δ' ἀφίξει νομάδας, οἳ πλεκτὰς στέγας
πεδάρσιοι ναίουσ' ἐπ' εὐκύκλοις ὄχοις, 710
ἑκηβόλοις τόξοισιν ἐξηρτημένοι·
οἷς μὴ πελάζειν, ἀλλ' ἁλιστόνοις πόδας
χρίμπτουσα ῥαχίαισιν ἐκπερᾶν χθόνα.
λαιᾶς δὲ χειρὸς οἱ σιδηροτέκτονες
οἰκοῦσι Χάλυβες, οὓς φυλάξασθαί σε χρή. 715
ἀνήμεροι γὰρ οὐδὲ πρόσπλαστοι ξένοις.

ἥξεις δ' Ὑβριστὴν ποταμὸν οὐ ψευδώνυμον,
ὃν μὴ περάσῃς, οὐ γὰρ εὔβατος περᾶν,
πρὶν ἂν πρὸς αὐτὸν Καύκασον μόλῃς, ὀρῶν
ὕψιστον, ἔνθα ποταμὸς ἐκφυσᾷ μένος   720
κροτάφων ἀπ' αὐτῶν. ἀστρογείτονας δὲ χρὴ
κορυφὰς ὑπερβάλλουσαν ἐς μεσημβρινὴν
βῆναι κέλευθον, ἔνθ' Ἀμαζόνων στρατὸν
ἥξει στυγάνορ', αἳ Θεμίσκυράν ποτε
κατοικιοῦσιν ἀμφὶ Θερμώδονθ', ἵνα   725
τραχεῖα πόντου Σαλμυδησία γνάθος
ἐχθρόξενος ναύταισι, μητρυιὰ νεῶν·
αὗταί σ' ὁδηγήσουσι καὶ μάλ' ἀσμένως.
ἰσθμὸν δ' ἐπ' αὐταῖς στενοπόροις λίμνης πύλαις
Κιμμερικὸν ἥξεις· ὃν θρασυσπλάγχνως σε χρὴ   730
λιποῦσαν αὐλῶν' ἐκπερᾶν Μαιωτικόν·
ἔσται δὲ θνητοῖς εἰσαεὶ λόγος μέγας
τῆς σῆς πορείας, Βόσπορος δ' ἐπώνυμος
κεκλήσεται. λιποῦσα δ' Εὐρώπης πέδον,
ἤπειρον ἥξεις Ἀσιάδ'. ἆρ' ὑμῖν δοκεῖ   735
ὁ τῶν θεῶν τύραννος ἐς τὰ πάνθ' ὁμῶς
βίαιος εἶναι; τῇδε γὰρ θνητῇ θεὸς
χρῄζων μιγῆναι, τάσδ' ἐπέρριψεν πλάνας.
πικροῦ δ' ἔκυρσας, ὦ κόρη, τῶν σῶν γάμων
μνηστῆρος. οὓς γὰρ νῦν ἀκήκοας λόγους,   740
εἶναι δόκει σοὶ μηδέπω 'ν προοιμίοις.

ΙΩ.

ἰώ μοί μοι, ἒ ἔ.

ΠΡΟΜΗΘΕΥΣ.

σὺ δ' αὖ κέκραγας κἀναμυχθίζει· τί που
δράσεις, ὅταν τὰ λοιπὰ πυνθάνῃ κακά;

ΠΡΟΜΗΘΕΥΣ ΔΕΣΜΩΤΗΣ.

ΧΟΡΟΣ.
ἦ γάρ τι λοιπὸν τῇδε πημάτων ἐρεῖς; 745
ΠΡΟΜΗΘΕΥΣ.
δυσχείμερόν γε πέλαγος ἀτηρᾶς δύης.
ΙΩ.
τί δῆτ᾽ ἐμοὶ ζῆν κέρδος, ἀλλ᾽ οὐκ ἐν τάχει
ἔῤῥιψ᾽ ἐμαυτὴν τῆσδ᾽ ἀπὸ στύφλου πέτρας,
ὅπως πέδῳ σκήψασα τῶν πάντων πόνων
ἀπηλλάγην; κρεῖσσον γὰρ εἰσάπαξ θανεῖν 750
ἢ τὰς ἁπάσας ἡμέρας πάσχειν κακῶς.
ΠΡΟΜΗΘΕΥΣ.
ἦ δυσπετῶς ἂν τοὺς ἐμοὺς ἄθλους φέροις,
ὅτῳ θανεῖν μέν ἐστιν οὐ πεπρωμένον·
αὕτη γὰρ ἦν ἂν πημάτων ἀπαλλαγή·
νῦν δ᾽ οὐδέν ἐστι τέρμα μοι προκείμενον 755
μόχθων, πρὶν ἂν Ζεὺς ἐκπέσῃ τυραννίδος.
ΙΩ.
ἦ γάρ ποτ᾽ ἐστὶν ἐκπεσεῖν ἀρχῆς Δία;
ΠΡΟΜΗΘΕΥΣ.
ἥδοι᾽ ἄν, οἶμαι, τήνδ᾽ ἰδοῦσα συμφοράν.
ΙΩ.
πῶς δ᾽ οὐκ ἄν, ἥτις ἐκ Διὸς πάσχω κακῶς;
ΠΡΟΜΗΘΕΥΣ.
ὡς τοίνυν ὄντων τῶνδέ σοι μαθεῖν πάρα. 760
ΙΩ.
πρὸς τοῦ τύραννα σκῆπτρα συληθήσεται;
ΠΡΟΜΗΘΕΥΣ.
αὐτὸς πρὸς αὑτοῦ κενοφρόνων βουλευμάτων.
ΙΩ.
ποίῳ τρόπῳ; σήμηνον, εἰ μή τις βλάβη.

ΠΡΟΜΗΘΕΥΣ.
γαμεῖ γάμον τοιοῦτον ᾧ ποτ' ἀσχαλᾷ.
ΙΩ.
θέορτον, ἢ βρότειον; εἰ ῥητὸν, φράσον.   765
ΠΡΟΜΗΘΕΥΣ.
τί δ' ὅντιν'; οὐ γὰρ ῥητὸν αὐδᾶσθαι τάδε.
ΙΩ.
ἦ πρὸς δάμαρτος ἐξανίσταται θρόνων;
ΠΡΟΜΗΘΕΥΣ.
ἣ τέξεταί γε παῖδα φέρτερον πατρός.
ΙΩ.
οὐδ' ἔστιν αὐτῷ τῆσδ' ἀποστροφὴ τύχης;
ΠΡΟΜΗΘΕΥΣ.
οὐ δῆτα, πρὶν ἔγωγ' ἂν ἐκ δεσμῶν λυθείς,—   770
ΙΩ.
τίς οὖν ὁ λύσων σ' ἐστὶν ἄκοντος Διός;
ΠΡΟΜΗΘΕΥΣ.
τῶν σῶν τιν' αὐτὸν ἐκγόνων εἶναι χρεών.
ΙΩ.
πῶς εἶπας; ἦ 'μὸς παῖς σ' ἀπαλλάξει κακῶν;
ΠΡΟΜΗΘΕΥΣ.
τρίτος γε γένναν πρὸς δέχ' ἄλλαισιν γοναῖς.
ΙΩ.
ἥδ' οὐκ ἔτ' εὐξύμβλητος ἡ χρησμῳδία.   775
ΠΡΟΜΗΘΕΥΣ.
καὶ μηδὲ σαυτῆς ἐκμαθεῖν ζήτει πόνους.
ΙΩ.
μή μοι προτείνων κέρδος εἶτ' ἀποστέρει.

ΠΡΟΜΗΘΕΥΣ ΔΕΣΜΩΤΗΣ.

ΠΡΟΜΗΘΕΥΣ.
δυοῖν λόγοιν σε θατέρῳ δωρήσομαι.
ΙΩ.
ποίοιν πρόδειξον, αἵρεσίν τ' ἐμοὶ δίδου.
ΠΡΟΜΗΘΕΥΣ.
δίδωμ'· ἑλοῦ γὰρ, ἢ πόνων τὰ λοιπά σοι 780
φράσω σαφηνῶς, ἢ τὸν ἐκλύσοντ' ἐμέ.
ΧΟΡΟΣ.
τούτων σὺ τὴν μὲν τῇδε, τὴν δ' ἐμοὶ χάριν
θέσθαι θέλησον, μηδ' ἀτιμάσῃς λόγους·
καὶ τῇδε μὲν γέγωνε τὴν λοιπὴν πλάνην,
ἐμοὶ δὲ τὸν λύσοντα· τοῦτο γὰρ ποθῶ. 785
ΠΡΟΜΗΘΕΥΣ.
ἐπεὶ προθυμεῖσθ', οὐκ ἐναντιώσομαι
τὸ μὴ οὐ γεγωνεῖν πᾶν ὅσον προσχρῄζετε.
σοὶ πρῶτον, Ἰοῖ, πολύδονον πλάνην φράσω,
ἣν ἐγγράφου σὺ μνήμοσιν δέλτοις φρενῶν.
ὅταν περάσῃς ῥεῖθρον ἠπείρων ὅρον, 790
πρὸς ἀντολὰς φλογῶπας ἡλιοστιβεῖς * * *
πόντου περῶσα φλοῖσβον, ἔς τ' ἂν ἐξίκῃ
πρὸς Γοργόνεια πεδία Κισθήνης, ἵνα
αἱ Φορκίδες ναίουσι δηναιαὶ κόραι
τρεῖς κυκνόμορφοι, κοινὸν ὄμμ' ἐκτημέναι, 795
μονόδοντες, ἃς οὔθ' ἥλιος προσδέρκεται
ἀκτῖσιν οὔθ' ἡ νύκτερος μήνη ποτέ.
πέλας δ' ἀδελφαὶ τῶνδε τρεῖς κατάπτεροι,
δρακοντόμαλλοι Γοργόνες βροτοστυγεῖς,
ἃς θνητὸς οὐδεὶς εἰσιδὼν ἕξει πνοάς· 800
τοιοῦτο μέν σοι τοῦτο φρούριον λέγω.

ἄλλην δ' ἄκουσον δυσχερῆ θεωρίαν·
ὀξυστόμους γὰρ Ζηνὸς ἀκραγεῖς κύνας
γρῦπας φύλαξαι, τόν τε μουνῶπα στρατὸν
Ἀριμασπὸν ἱπποβάμον᾽, οἳ χρυσόρρυτον 805
οἰκοῦσιν ἀμφὶ νᾶμα Πλούτωνος πόρου·
τούτοις σὺ μὴ πέλαζε. τηλουρὸν δὲ γῆν
ἥξεις κελαινὸν φῦλον, οἳ πρὸς ἡλίου
ναίουσι πηγαῖς, ἔνθα ποταμὸς Αἰθίοψ.
τούτου παρ' ὄχθας ἕρφ᾽, ἕως ἂν ἐξίκῃ 810
καταβασμόν, ἔνθα Βυβλίνων ὀρῶν ἄπο
ἵησι σεπτὸν Νεῖλος εὔποτον ῥέος.
οὗτός σ' ὁδώσει τὴν τρίγωνον ἐς χθόνα
Νειλῶτιν, οὗ δὴ τὴν μακρὰν ἀποικίαν,
Ἰοῖ, πέπρωται σοί τε καὶ τέκνοις κτίσαι. 815
τῶν δ' εἴ τί σοι ψελλόν τε καὶ δυσεύρετον,
ἐπαναδίπλαζε, καὶ σαφῶς ἐκμάνθανε·
σχολὴ δὲ πλείων ἢ θέλω πάρεστί μοι.

ΧΟΡΟΣ.
εἰ μέν τι τῇδε λοιπὸν ἢ παρειμένον
ἔχεις γεγωνεῖν τῆς πολυφθόρου πλάνης, 820
λέγ᾽· εἰ δὲ πάντ' εἴρηκας, ἡμῖν αὖ χάριν
δὸς ἥντιν' αἰτούμεσθα, μέμνησαι δέ που.

ΠΡΟΜΗΘΕΥΣ.
τὸ πᾶν πορείας ἥδε τέρμ᾽ ἀκήκοεν.
ὅπως δ' ἂν εἰδῇ μὴ μάτην κλύουσά μου,
ἃ πρὶν μολεῖν δεῦρ' ἐκμεμόχθηκεν φράσω, 825
τεκμήριον τοῦτ᾽ αὐτὸ δοὺς μύθων ἐμῶν.
ὄχλον μὲν οὖν τὸν πλεῖστον ἐκλείψω λόγων,
πρὸς αὐτὸ δ᾽ εἶμι τέρμα σῶν πλανημάτων.

ἐπεὶ γὰρ ἦλθες πρὸς Μολοσσὰ γάπεδα,
τὴν αἰπύνωτόν τ' ἀμφὶ Δωδώνην, ἵνα 830
μαντεῖα θῶκός τ' ἐστὶ Θεσπρωτοῦ Διὸς,
τέρας τ' ἄπιστον, αἱ προσήγοροι δρύες,
ὑφ' ὧν σὺ λαμπρῶς κοὐδὲν αἰνικτηρίως
προσηγορεύθης ἡ Διὸς κλεινὴ δάμαρ
μέλλουσ' ἔσεσθ', εἴ τῶνδε προσσαίνει σέ τι, 835
ἐντεῦθεν οἰστρήσασα τὴν παρακτίαν
κέλευθον ᾖξας πρὸς μέγαν κόλπον Ῥέας,
ἀφ' οὗ παλιμπλάγκτοισι χειμάζει δρόμοις·
χρόνον δὲ τὸν μέλλοντα πόντιος μυχὸς,
σαφῶς ἐπίστασ', Ἰόνιος κεκλήσεται, 840
τῆς σῆς πορείας μνῆμα τοῖς πᾶσιν βροτοῖς.
σημεῖά σοι τάδ' ἐστὶ τῆς ἐμῆς φρενὸς,
ὡς δέρκεται πλέον τι τοῦ πεφασμένου.
τὰ λοιπὰ δ' ὑμῖν τῇδέ τ' ἐς κοινὸν φράσω,
ἐς ταυτὸν ἐλθὼν τῶν πάλαι λόγων ἴχνος. 845
ἔστιν πόλις Κάνωβος ἐσχάτη χθονὸς,
Νείλου πρὸς αὐτῷ στόματι καὶ προσχώματι·
ἐνταῦθα δή σε Ζεὺς τίθησιν ἔμφρονα,
ἐπαφῶν ἀταρβεῖ χειρὶ καὶ θιγὼν μόνον.
ἐπώνυμον δὲ τῶν Διὸς γεννημάτων 850
τέξεις κελαινὸν Ἔπαφον· ὃς καρπώσεται
ὅσην πλατύῤῥους Νεῖλος ἀρδεύει χθόνα·
πέμπτη δ' ἀπ' αὐτοῦ γέννα πεντηκοντάπαις
πάλιν πρὸς Ἄργος οὐχ ἑκοῦσ' ἐλεύσεται
θηλύσπορος, φεύγουσα συγγενῆ γάμον 855
ἀνεψιῶν· οἱ δ' ἐπτοημένοι φρένας,
κίρκοι πελειῶν οὐ μακρὰν λελειμμένοι,

ἥξουσι θηρεύσοντες οὐ θηρασίμους
γάμους, φθόνον δὲ σωμάτων ἕξει θεός·
Πελασγία δὲ δέξεται, θηλυκτόνῳ 860
Ἄρει δαμέντων νυκτιφρουρήτῳ θράσει·
γυνὴ γὰρ ἄνδρ᾽ ἕκαστον αἰῶνος στερεῖ,
δίθηκτον ἐν σφαγαῖσι βάψασα ξίφος·
τοιάδ᾽ ἐπ᾽ ἐχθροὺς τοὺς ἐμοὺς ἔλθοι Κύπρις.
μίαν δὲ παίδων ἵμερος θέλξει τὸ μὴ 865
κτεῖναι ξύνευνον, ἀλλ᾽ ἀπαμβλυνθήσεται
γνώμην· δυοῖν δὲ θάτερον βουλήσεται,
κλύειν ἄναλκις μᾶλλον ἢ μιαιφόνος·
αὕτη κατ᾽ Ἄργος βασιλικὸν τέξει γένος.
μακροῦ λόγου δεῖ ταῦτ᾽ ἐπεξελθεῖν τορῶς. 870
σπορᾶς γε μὴν ἐκ τῆσδε φύσεται θρασὺς
τόξοισι κλεινός, ὃς πόνων ἐκ τῶνδ᾽ ἐμὲ
λύσει. τοιόνδε χρησμὸν ἡ παλαιγενὴς
μήτηρ ἐμοὶ διῆλθε Τιτανὶς Θέμις·
ὅπως δὲ χὤπῃ, ταῦτα δεῖ μακροῦ χρόνου 875
εἰπεῖν, σύ τ᾽ οὐδὲν ἐκμαθοῦσα κερδανεῖς.

ΙΩ.
ἐλελεῦ ἐλελεῦ, ὑπό μ᾽ αὖ σφάκελος
καὶ φρενοπληγεῖς μανίαι θάλπουσ᾽,
οἴστρου δ᾽ ἄρδις χρίει μ᾽ ἄπυρος· 880
κραδία δὲ φόβῳ φρένα λακτίζει.
τροχοδινεῖται δ᾽ ὄμμαθ᾽ ἑλίγδην,
ἔξω δὲ δρόμου φέρομαι λύσσης
πνεύματι μάργῳ, γλώσσης ἀκρατής·
θολεροὶ δὲ λόγοι παίουσ᾽ εἰκῇ 885
στυγνῆς πρὸς κύμασιν ἄτης.

ΠΡΟΜΗΘΕΥΣ ΔΕΣΜΩΤΗΣ.

ΧΟΡΟΣ.

ἦ σοφὸς ἦ σοφὸς ὃς
πρῶτος ἐν γνώμᾳ τόδ' ἐβάστασε καὶ γλώσσᾳ διε-
    μυθολόγησεν,
ὡς τὸ κηδεῦσαι καθ' ἑαυτὸν ἀριστεύει μακρῷ· 890
καὶ μήτε τῶν πλούτῳ διαθρυπτομένων
μήτε τῶν γέννᾳ μεγαλυνομένων
ὄντα χερνήταν ἐραστεῦσαι γάμων.
μήποτε μήποτέ μ', ὦ
* * * Μοῖραι λεχέων Διὸς εὐνάτειραν ἴδοισθε
            πέλουσαν· 895
μηδὲ πλαθείην γαμέτᾳ τινὶ τῶν ἐξ οὐρανοῦ.
ταρβῶ γὰρ ἀστεργάνορα παρθενίαν
εἰσορῶσ' Ἰοῦς μέγα δαπτομέναν
δυσπλάνοις Ἥρας ἀλατείαις πόνων. 900
ἐμοὶ δ' ὅτι μὲν ὁμαλὸς ὁ γάμος,
ἄφοβος, οὐ δέδια, μὴ δὲ κρεισσόνων θεῶν
ἔρως ἄφυκτον ὄμμα προσδράκοι με.
ἀπόλεμος ὅδε·γ' ὁ πόλεμος, ἄπορα
πόριμος· οὐδ' ἔχω τίς ἂν γενοίμαν. 905
τὰν Διὸς γὰρ οὐχ ὁρῶ
μῆτιν ὅπα φύγοιμ' ἄν.

ΠΡΟΜΗΘΕΥΣ.

ἦ μὴν ἔτι Ζεὺς, καίπερ αὐθάδης φρενῶν,
ἔσται ταπεινὸς, οἷον ἐξαρτύεται
γάμον γαμεῖν· ὃς αὐτὸν ἐκ τυραννίδος
θρόνων τ' ἄϊστον ἐκβαλεῖ· πατρὸς δ' ἀρὰ 910
Κρόνου τότ' ἤδη παντελῶς κρανθήσεται,

        887 — 893. = 894 — 900.

ἣν ἐκπιτνῶν ἠρᾶτο δηναιῶν θρόνων.
τοιῶνδε μόχθων ἐκτροπὴν οὐδεὶς θεῶν
δύναιτ' ἂν αὐτῷ πλὴν ἐμοῦ δεῖξαι σαφῶς.
ἐγὼ τάδ' οἶδα χᾧ τρόπῳ. πρὸς ταῦτα νῦν   915
θαρσῶν καθήσθω τοῖς πεδαρσίοις κτύποις
πιστός, τινάσσων χερσὶ πυρπνόον βέλος.
οὐδὲν γὰρ αὐτῷ ταῦτ' ἐπαρκέσει τὸ μὴ οὐ
πεσεῖν ἀτίμως πτώματ' οὐκ ἀνασχετά·
τοῖον παλαιστὴν νῦν παρασκευάζεται   920
ἐπ' αὐτὸς αὑτῷ, δυσμαχώτατον τέρας·
ὃς δὴ κεραυνοῦ κρείσσον' εὑρήσει φλόγα,
βροντῆς θ' ὑπερβάλλοντα καρτερὸν κτύπον·
θαλασσίαν τε γῆς τινάκτειραν νόσον
τρίαιναν, αἰχμὴν τὴν Ποσειδῶνος, σκεδᾷ.   925
πταίσας δὲ τῷδε πρὸς κακῷ, μαθήσεται
ὅσον τό τ' ἄρχειν καὶ τὸ δουλεύειν δίχα.

XOPOΣ.
σύ θην ἃ χρῄζεις, ταῦτ' ἐπιγλωσσᾷ Διός.

ΠΡΟΜΗΘΕΥΣ.
ἅπερ τελεῖται, πρὸς δ' ἃ βούλομαι λέγω.

XOPOΣ.
καὶ προσδοκᾶν χρὴ δεσπόσειν Ζηνὸς τινά;   930

ΠΡΟΜΗΘΕΥΣ.
καὶ τῶνδέ γ' ἕξει δυσλοφωτέρους πόνους.

XOPOΣ.
πῶς δ' οὐχὶ ταρβεῖς τοιάδ' ἐκρίπτων ἔπη;

ΠΡΟΜΗΘΕΥΣ.
τί δ' ἂν φοβοίμην, ᾧ θανεῖν οὐ μόρσιμον;

ΠΡΟΜΗΘΕΥΣ ΔΕΣΜΩΤΗΣ. 43

ΧΟΡΟΣ.
ἀλλ' ἆθλον ἄν σοι τοῦδέ γ' ἀλγίω πόροι.
ΠΡΟΜΗΘΕΥΣ.
ὁ δ' οὖν ποιείτω· πάντα προσδοκητά μοι. 935
ΧΟΡΟΣ.
οἱ προσκυνοῦντες τὴν Ἀδράστειαν σοφοί.
ΠΡΟΜΗΘΕΥΣ.
σέβου, προσεύχου, θῶπτε τὸν κρατοῦντ' ἀεί.
ἐμοὶ δ' ἔλασσον Ζηνὸς ἢ μηδὲν μέλει.
δράτω, κρατείτω τόνδε τὸν βραχὺν χρόνον,
ὅπως θέλει· δαρὸν γὰρ οὐκ ἄρξει θεοῖς. 940
ἀλλ' εἰσορῶ γὰρ τόνδε τὸν Διὸς τρόχιν,
τὸν τοῦ τυράννου τοῦ νέου διάκονον·
πάντως τι καινὸν ἀγγελῶν ἐλήλυθε.

ΕΡΜΗΣ.
σὲ τὸν σοφιστὴν, τὸν πικρῶς ὑπέρπικρον,
τὸν ἐξαμαρτόντ' εἰς θεοὺς ἐφημέροις 945
πορόντα τιμὰς, τὸν πυρὸς κλέπτην λέγω·
πατὴρ ἄνωγέ σ' οὕστινας κομπεῖς γάμους
αὐδᾶν, πρὸς ὧν τ' ἐκεῖνος ἐκπίπτει κράτους·
καὶ ταῦτα μέντοι μηδὲν αἰνικτηρίως,
ἀλλ' αὔθ' ἕκαστ' ἔκφραζε· μηδέ μοι διπλᾶς 950
ὁδοὺς, Προμηθεῦ, προσβάλῃς· ὁρᾷς δ' ὅτι
Ζεὺς τοῖς τοιούτοις οὐχὶ μαλθακίζεται.

ΠΡΟΜΗΘΕΥΣ.
σεμνόστομός γε καὶ φρονήματος πλέως
ὁ μῦθός ἐστιν, ὡς θεῶν ὑπηρέτου.
νέον νέοι κρατεῖτε καὶ δοκεῖτε δὴ 955
ναίειν ἀπενθῆ πέργαμ'· οὐκ ἐκ τῶνδ' ἐγὼ

δισσοὺς τυράννους ἐκπεσόντας ἠσθόμην;
τρίτον δὲ τὸν νῦν κοιρανοῦντ' ἐπόψομαι
αἴσχιστα καὶ τάχιστα. μή τί σοι δοκῶ
ταρβεῖν ὑποπτήσσειν τε τοὺς νέους θεούς;
πολλοῦ γε καὶ τοῦ παντὸς ἐλλείπω. σὺ δὲ
κέλευθον ἥνπερ ἦλθες ἐγκόνει πάλιν·
πεύσει γὰρ οὐδὲν ὧν ἀνιστορεῖς ἐμέ.

ΕΡΜΗΣ.
τοιοῖσδε μέντοι καὶ πρὶν αὐθαδίσμασιν
ἐς τάσδε σαυτὸν πημονὰς καθώρμισας.

ΠΡΟΜΗΘΕΥΣ.
τῆς σῆς λατρείας τὴν ἐμὴν δυσπραξίαν,
σαφῶς ἐπίστασ', οὐκ ἂν ἀλλάξαιμ' ἐγώ.
κρεῖσσον γὰρ οἶμαι τῇδε λατρεύειν πέτρᾳ
ἢ πατρὶ φῦναι Ζηνὶ πιστὸν ἄγγελον.
οὕτως ὑβρίζειν τοὺς ὑβρίζοντας χρεών.

ΕΡΜΗΣ.
χλιδᾶν ἔοικας τοῖς παροῦσι πράγμασι.

ΠΡΟΜΗΘΕΥΣ.
χλιδῶ; χλιδῶντας ὧδε τοὺς ἐμοὺς ἐγὼ
ἐχθροὺς ἴδοιμι· καὶ σὲ δ' ἐν τούτοις λέγω.

ΕΡΜΗΣ.
ἦ κἀμὲ γάρ τι ξυμφοραῖς ἐπαιτιᾷ;

ΠΡΟΜΗΘΕΥΣ.
ἁπλῷ λόγῳ τοὺς πάντας ἐχθαίρω θεούς,
ὅσοι παθόντες εὖ κακοῦσί μ' ἐκδίκως.

ΕΡΜΗΣ.
κλύω σ' ἐγὼ μεμηνότ' οὐ σμικρὰν νόσον

ΠΡΟΜΗΘΕΥΣ ΔΕΣΜΩΤΗΣ.

ΠΡΟΜΗΘΕΥΣ.
νοσοῖμ' ἄν, εἰ νόσημα τοὺς ἐχθροὺς στυγεῖν.
ΕΡΜΗΣ.
εἴης φορητὸς οὐκ ἄν, εἰ πράσσοις καλῶς.
ΠΡΟΜΗΘΕΥΣ.
ὤμοι. 980
ΕΡΜΗΣ.
τόδε Ζεὺς τοὔπος οὐκ ἐπίσταται.
ΠΡΟΜΗΘΕΥΣ.
ἀλλ' ἐκδιδάσκει πάνθ' ὁ γηράσκων χρόνος.
ΕΡΜΗΣ.
καὶ μὴν σύ γ' οὔπω σωφρονεῖν ἐπίστασαι.
ΠΡΟΜΗΘΕΥΣ.
σὲ γὰρ προσηύδων οὐκ ἂν ὄνθ' ὑπηρέτην.
ΕΡΜΗΣ.
ἐρεῖν ἔοικας οὐδὲν ὧν χρῄζει πατήρ.
ΠΡΟΜΗΘΕΥΣ.
καὶ μὴν ὀφείλων γ' ἂν τίνοιμ' αὐτῷ χάριν. 985
ΕΡΜΗΣ.
ἐκερτόμησας δῆθεν ὡς παῖδ' ὄντα με.
ΠΡΟΜΗΘΕΥΣ.
οὐ γὰρ σὺ παῖς τε κἄτι τοῦδ' ἀνούστερος,
εἰ προσδοκᾷς ἐμοῦ τι πευσεῖσθαι πάρα;
οὐκ ἔστιν αἴκισμ' οὐδὲ μηχάνημ', ὅτῳ
προτρέψεταί με Ζεὺς γεγωνῆσαι τάδε, 990
πρὶν ἂν χαλασθῇ δεσμὰ λυμαντήρια.
πρὸς ταῦτα ῥιπτέσθω μὲν αἰθαλοῦσσα φλὸξ,
λευκοπτέρῳ δὲ νιφάδι καὶ βροντήμασι
χθονίοις κυκάτω πάντα καὶ ταρασσέτω·

γνάμψει γὰρ οὐδὲν τῶνδέ μ' ὥστε καὶ φράσαι 995
πρὸς οὗ χρεών νιν ἐκπεσεῖν τυραννίδος.

ΕΡΜΗΣ.

ὅρα νυν εἴ σοι ταῦτ' ἀρωγὰ φαίνεται.

ΠΡΟΜΗΘΕΥΣ.

ὦπται πάλαι δὴ καὶ βεβούλευται τάδε.

ΕΡΜΗΣ.

τόλμησον, ὦ μάταιε, τόλμησόν ποτε
πρὸς τὰς παρούσας πημονὰς ὀρθῶς φρονεῖν. 1000

ΠΡΟΜΗΘΕΥΣ.

ὀχλεῖς μάτην με, κῦμ' ὅπως, παρηγορῶν.
εἰσελθέτω σε μήποθ', ὡς ἐγὼ Διὸς
γνώμην φοβηθεὶς θηλύνους γενήσομαι,
καὶ λιπαρήσω τὸν μέγα στυγούμενον
γυναικομίμοις ὑπτιάσμασιν χερῶν 1005
λῦσαί με δεσμῶν τῶνδε· τοῦ παντὸς δέω.

ΕΡΜΗΣ.

λέγων ἔοικα πολλὰ καὶ μάτην ἐρεῖν·
τέγγει γὰρ οὐδὲν οὐδὲ μαλθάσσει κέαρ
λιταῖς· δακὼν δὲ στόμιον, ὡς νεοζυγὴς
πῶλος, βιάζει καὶ πρὸς ἡνίας μάχει. 1010
ἀτὰρ σφοδρύνει γ' ἀσθενεῖ σοφίσματι.
αὐθαδία γὰρ τῷ φρονοῦντι μὴ καλῶς
αὐτὴ καθ' αὑτὴν οὐδενὸς μεῖον σθένει.
σκέψαι δ', ἐὰν μὴ τοῖς ἐμοῖς πεισθῇς λόγοις,
οἷός σε χειμὼν καὶ κακῶν τρικυμία 1015
ἔπεισ' ἄφυκτος· πρῶτα μὲν γὰρ ὀκρίδα
φάραγγα βροντῇ καὶ κεραυνίᾳ φλογὶ
πατὴρ σπαράξει τήνδε, καὶ κρύψει δέμας

τὸ σὸν, πετραία δ' ἀγκάλη σε βαστάσει.
μακρὸν δὲ μῆκος ἐκτελευτήσας χρόνου
ἄψοῤῥον ἥξεις ἐς φάος· Διὸς δέ τοι
πτηνὸς κύων δαφοινὸς αἰετὸς λάβρως
διαρταμήσει σώματος μέγα ῥάκος,
ἄκλητος ἕρπων δαιταλεὺς πανήμερος,
κελαινόβρωτον δ' ἧπαρ ἐκθοινήσεται.
τοιοῦδε μόχθου τέρμα μή τι προσδόκα,
πρὶν ἂν θεῶν τις διάδοχος τῶν σῶν πόνων
φανῇ, θελήσῃ τ' εἰς ἀναύγητον μολεῖν
Ἅιδην κνεφαῖά τ' ἀμφὶ Ταρτάρου βάθη.
πρὸς ταῦτα βούλευ'· ὡς ὅδ' οὐ πεπλασμένος
ὁ κόμπος, ἀλλὰ καὶ λίαν εἰρημένος·
ψευδηγορεῖν γὰρ οὐκ ἐπίσταται στόμα
τὸ δῖον, ἀλλὰ πᾶν ἔπος τελεῖ. σὺ δὲ
πάπταινε καὶ φρόντιζε, μηδ' αὐθαδίαν
εὐβουλίας ἀμείνον' ἡγήσῃ ποτέ.

ΧΟΡΟΣ.

ἡμῖν μὲν Ἑρμῆς οὐκ ἄκαιρα φαίνεται
λέγειν· ἄνωγε γάρ σε τὴν αὐθαδίαν
μεθέντ' ἐρευνᾶν τὴν σοφὴν εὐβουλίαν.
πείθου· σοφῷ γὰρ αἰσχρὸν ἐξαμαρτάνειν.

ΠΡΟΜΗΘΕΥΣ.

εἰδότι τοί μοι τάσδ' ἀγγελίας
ὅδ' ἐθώϋξεν, πάσχειν δὲ κακῶς
ἐχθρὸν ὑπ' ἐχθρῶν οὐδὲν ἀεικές.
πρὸς ταῦτ' ἐπ' ἐμοὶ ῥιπτέσθω μὲν
πυρὸς ἀμφήκης βόστρυχος, αἰθὴρ δ'
ἐρεθιζέσθω

βροντῇ σφακέλῳ τ' ἀγρίων ἀνέμων·
χθόνα δ' ἐκ πυθμένων αὐταῖς ῥίζαις
πνεῦμα κραδαίνοι,
κῦμα δὲ πόντου τραχεῖ ῥοθίῳ
ξυγχώσειεν τῶν τ' οὐρανίων
ἄστρων διόδους, ἔς τε κελαινὸν
Τάρταρον ἄρδην ῥίψειε δέμας
τοὐμὸν ἀνάγκης στερραῖς δίναις
πάντως ἐμέ γ' οὐ θανατώσει.

ΕΡΜΗΣ.
τοιάδε μέντοι τῶν φρενοπλήκτων
βουλεύματ' ἔπη τ' ἐστὶν ἀκοῦσαι.
τί γὰρ ἐλλείπει μὴ παραπαίειν
ἡ τοῦδε τύχη; τί χαλᾷ μανιῶν;
ἀλλ' οὖν ὑμεῖς γ' αἱ πημοσύναις
ξυγκάμνουσαι ταῖς τοῦδε, τόπων
μετά που χωρεῖτ' ἐκ τῶνδε θοῶς·
μὴ φρένας ὑμῶν ἠλιθιώσῃ
βροντῆς μύκημ' ἀτέραμνον.

ΧΟΡΟΣ.
ἄλλο τι φώνει καὶ παραμυθοῦ μ'
ὅ τι καὶ πείσεις· οὐ γὰρ δή που
τοῦτό γε τλητὸν παρέσυρας ἔπος.
πῶς με κελεύεις κακότητ' ἀσκεῖν;
μετὰ τοῦδ' ὅ τι χρὴ πάσχειν ἐθέλω·
τοὺς προδότας γὰρ μισεῖν ἔμαθον,
κοὐκ ἔστι νόσος
τῆσδ' ἥντιν' ἀπέπτυσα μᾶλλον.

ΠΡΟΜΗΘΕΥΣ ΔΕΣΜΩΤΗΣ. 49

ΕΡΜΗΣ.

ἀλλ' οὖν μέμνησθ' ἅτ' ἐγὼ προλέγω·
μηδὲ πρὸς ἄτης θηραθεῖσαι
μέμψησθε τύχην, μηδέ ποτ' εἴπηθ'
ὡς Ζεὺς ὑμᾶς εἰς ἀπρόοπτον
πῆμ' εἰσέβαλεν· 1075
μὴ δῆτ', αὐταὶ δ' ὑμᾶς αὐτάς.
εἰδυῖαι γὰρ κοὐκ ἐξαίφνης
οὐδὲ λαθραίως
εἰς ἀπέραντον δίκτυον ἄτης
ἐμπλεχθήσεσθ' ὑπ' ἀνοίας.

ΠΡΟΜΗΘΕΥΣ.

καὶ μὴν ἔργῳ κοὐκ ἔτι μύθῳ 1080
χθὼν σεσάλευται·
βρυχία δ' ἠχὼ παραμυκᾶται
βροντῆς, ἕλικες δ' ἐκλάμπουσι
στεροπῆς ζάπυροι,
στρόμβοι δὲ κόνιν εἱλίσσουσι· 1085
σκιρτᾷ δ' ἀνέμων πνεύματα πάντων
εἰς ἄλληλα
στάσιν ἀντίπνουν ἀποδεικνύμενα·
ξυντετάρακται δ' αἰθὴρ πόντῳ.
τοιάδ' ἐπ' ἐμοὶ ῥιπὴ διόθεν
τεύχουσα φόβον στείχει φανερῶς. 1090
ὦ μητρὸς ἐμῆς σέβας, ὦ πάντων
αἰθὴρ κοινὸν φάος εἱλίσσων,
ἐσορᾷς μ' ὡς ἔκδικα πάσχω.

NOTES.

NOTES.

[Mt. = Matthiæ's Gram., 2d edition; and K., Kühner's Middle Gram., Andover translation.]

1.) On the persons of the drama.

Kratos and Bia both appeared on the stage, but the latter was a mute. It is not improbable that an image representing Prometheus was fastened to the rocks, or within a fissure of rock, behind which an actor was stationed. This play requires but two actors, one of whom played the parts of Kratos, Okeanus, Io, and Hermes, and the other those of Hephæstus and Prometheus. Io appeared on the stage probably as a female, and yet as βουκερώς.

2.) On the arguments. — *Arg.* 1. The lost play of Sophocles here spoken of must have been called Kolchides from its chorus, and have related to the adventures of the Argonauts at the palace of Æetes, including the death of Apsyrtus, of which he chose to make that the scene. A line from this play, still preserved,

ὑμεῖς μὲν οὐκ ἄρ' ἦστε τὸν Προμηθέα,

may have introduced the episode of which the argument makes mention. — *Arg.* 2. The inferior age of this writer is shown by λέγει ἵνα πείσῃ, with the sense here belonging to these words; by τέξει, more poetic for τέξεται, the usual prose form; and by μὴ βουλόμενον, for οὐ βουλόμενον.

2. Σκύθην ἐς οἶμον. Σκύθης is used adjectively, here and in

v. 417, like many other nouns, especially national names. οἶμος is rendered *tract, region,* by Passow. The nearest approach to this sense is found in the Homeric use of the word to denote the parallel plates of a shield, and in its application to the stripes or zones of which a shield might be composed. Schömann therefore understands it of Scythia, as the strip or long tract of land stretching across the northern parts of the world. Or Σκύθης οἶμος, without implying the existence of a path, may be regarded as an ornamental expression for *Scythia,* considered as the region where their track lay. The word is again used in v. 394. Comp. 281, where the air is called the πόρος of birds, i. e. *the place through which they pass.* —— ἄβατον. Another reading, ἄβροτον, cited by several ancient grammarians, is preferred by Blomf. It seems, however, to have less authority than the reading of the MSS., and may have sprung from the conjecture of some one, who thought that there was an inconsistency between οἶμον and ἄβατον.

3. In abrupt addresses, where δὲ and a vocative occur, the vocative is put first, and a personal pronoun with δὲ succeeds. Comp. Mt. § 312. 3.— The order is, χρὴ ἐπιστολὰς μέλειν σοί. ἐπιστολὰς answers in sense and derivation to *mandata,* ἐφετμή.

5. λεωργὸς Hesychius defines by κακοῦργος, πανοῦργος, ἀνδροφόνος. Xenophon, Mem. I. 3. 9, uses this word with θερμουργός, *bold, boldly wicked.* Herm. compares ῥᾳδιουργός.

6. ἀδαμαντίνων, *of adamant* or *hard iron.* ἀδαμαντόδετος, 148, 426, means *produced by iron bonds.* ἀδάμας, first an epithet of some metal, came to mean especially *hard iron, steel.*

7. ἄνθος, *that which is ornamental, choice,* or *honorable,* as the flower is to the plant. Here it answers to γέρας, of v. 38, and to τιμαὶ as used Alcest. 30, in the sense of a *choice gift, prerogatives.*

11. στέργειν. This word, like ἀγαπᾶν, often answers to

acquiesce in, be content with, and so Blomf. takes it here; but the sense *to love* can be admitted, as φιλανθρώπου needs a contrast in the preceding clause. He had loved men; but now he must learn to love Jupiter's government. So Wellauer and J. Jones in Class. Journ. 17. 31.

13. οὐδὲν ἐμποδὼν ἔτι, *there is nothing before you,* or *requiring your attention.* ἐμποδὼν means, 1. *upon* or *before the feet, present, at hand ;* 2. *in the way ;* which is the most common shade of meaning. Blomf. renders it somewhat loosely *reliquum,* but ἔτι contains that idea.

14. συγγενῆ denotes nothing more than that both belonged to the race of the Gods.

15. φάραγξ. Blomf. *vallis inter montium præerupta,* i. e. a *cleft, chasm, gorge.* But the word, wherever used in this play, unless perhaps in v. 142, denotes a *cliff* or *rock* bordering such a chasm. Otherwise the expressions ὤχμασεν ἐν φάραγγι, v. 618, σπαράξει φάραγγα, v. 1017, and δῆσαι πρὸς φάραγγι of the present line, would have no sense.

16. σχεθεῖν Elmsley regards as an aorist (comp. his note on Heraclidæ 272), and it is here accented as such. The sense requires that an aorist infin. expressive of a single action or event, and not a present expressive of continued, or repeated, or unfinished action, should be used.

17. ἐξωριάζειν. This word is not elsewhere found. Several critics would substitute εὐωριάζειν, a word of the same sense, credited to Sophocles by Hesychius.

21. φωνήν. ὄψει of the next verse implies ἀκούσει, — an instance of the figure called zeugma. K. § 346. 3. —— του. Griffiths remarks that only six instances occur in Æschylus of this form and τῳ or τῴ for the longer forms of τις and τίς.

22. σταθευτός, *slightly burnt, scorched.* σταθεύειν γὰρ, says the Schol., τὸ κατ' ὀλίγον ὀπτᾶν.

27. λωφήσων. It is very rare that λωφάω is active, as here. An instance may be found in Apol. Rhod. 4. 1418.

λήγω is now and then active, but usually neuter. The Schol. on that passage, Suidas, Hesychius, and the Etym. Mag., concur in assigning as the original meaning of this verb *to remove a burden from the neck*, and in deriving it from λόφος. If they are right, the metaphor corresponds with the literal meaning of ἀχθηδών, *burdensomeness*. —— οὐ πέφυκέ πω. Hercules, who was to deliver Prometheus, is not meant by Vulcan, as the Gods knew nothing of this event, but the expression is general; and the poet chose the language with allusion to what should happen.

28. τοιαῦτ᾽ ἀπηύρω, *such good you got.* This is the only instance where the forms belonging to ἀπαυράω take the meaning appropriate to ἐπαυρίσκομαι, *I enjoy, reap advantage.* Elmsley would therefore read ἐπηύρου. Buttmann (Lexil. No. 22) thinks, that, as ἀπαυράω in the active means *take from*, a middle form, like the one in question, may mean *take to one's self from, gain, enjoy.* This remark defends the vulgar reading.

39. τοι is used here, as it often is, to introduce a received truth or *locus communis*. It answers to *you know*. —— δεινόν, *powerful in its influence on the feelings*, a strong bond. Comp. Electr. 770.

41. δειμαίνεις alludes to δεινόν, v. 39. Griffiths.

45. χειρωναξία, *handicraft*, a word used only by Æschylus, from χειρῶναξ, *workmaster*.

46. ὡς ἁπλῷ λόγῳ, sc. εἰπεῖν, *to speak in a simple* or openhearted *word*, i. e. to tell the simple truth.

49. The reading of the MSS. here, ἅπαντ᾽ ἐπράχθη, is of difficult explanation, as may be seen by reading the twisted interpretations of the Scholiasts. Schütz renders the passage "*omnia diis sunt acquisita* praeterquam imperare"; Scholefield, "*omnia diis fieri solent*, i. e. possunt," κ. τ. λ. But the position of πλὴν requires that θεοῖσι be taken with κοιρανεῖν. The words may be rendered, "you acquired (i. e. under the new regime) every thing but dominion over the

Gods; and no one has this (is *free*, supreme), except Jupiter. Your lot, therefore, is not so bad." But the sense elicited from these words is so oracular at the best, that in this third edition I have followed Stanley's elegant conjecture approved by Hermann and received by Blomf. and by Schömann; which accords exceedingly well with the next line, and with the character of the speaker; *all things are onerous but to reign over the Gods; for no one is free save Jove:* i. e. there is toil in every condition except that of the supreme ruler.

55. νιν = αὐτά, referring to ψάλια, which properly denotes *curb-chain to a bit*, but here *arm-chain, handcuff*, and seems to be cognate with ψέλλιον, *bracelet*.

57. ματᾷ Blomf. and Well. render with a Schol. by *cunctor*. Hesychius ματᾷ, διατρίβει, χρονίζει. But the interpretation of another Schol., οὐ μάτην γίγνεται, *has accomplished its purpose*, is good. This word has the first sense in Sept. ad Theb. 37, and the second in Eumenid. 142.

62. μάθῃ ὤν, *may learn that he is;* but μάθῃ εἶναι, *may learn to be, how to be.* K. § 311. Comp. 1068. ——— σοφιστής = τεχνίτης. The Scholia Veneta on Il. xv. 410, cited by Blomf., say, οἱ παλαιοὶ (τοὺς τεχνίτας) σοφιστὰς ἐκάλουν.

68. ὅπως. ὅρα or σκόπει is to be supplied before the conjunction. Comp. Mt. § 519. 7; K. § 330. 6, R. 4.

76. διατόρους Schütz renders *perforatas*, i. e. *having holes in them*, through which the nails that entered the rock were driven. But the active meaning, *piercing* (i. e. piercing the rocks), is far to be preferred. Comp. 181, where fear is called διάτορος.

77. ὁ ἐπιτιμητής, *the censurer*, or *censor*.

81. ἀμφίβληστρον is *any thing thrown around*, as *clothing*, *a net;* here, *chain-work*. — On this word κώλοισιν depends.

86, 87. προμηθέως, *of a man of foresight* or *forethought*. Æsch. uses the word as an adj., Suppl. 681 (700), where it means *having foresight* or *forethought, provident*. ——— σε δεῖ. δεῖ takes a dative or accusative of a person, but more commonly the first. K. § 279. 4, R. 4.——ὅτῳ follows προμηθέως. The construction is, You have need of *a man able to devise in what way.* —— τύχης is the common reading of the edd. instead of τέχνης, which latter, as the more exquisite reading and supported by a number of MSS., Blomf. and Well. justly prefer. τέχνη here, like our word *contrivance,* means *the thing contrived,* the skilfully fastened chains. Comp. μηχανή, *art, contrivance,* and *machine.*

90. γέλασμα. Where the Greeks used this metaphor in relation to the waves, the sea, or the shore, they usually denoted by it *something heard,* viz. *the gentle dash of waves in a calm,* e. g. upon the shore; a sound resembling *laughter* in itself, and associated in thought with a glad state of mind. Comp. the farrago of examples in Blomfield's gloss. But sometimes, as here, it seems to be spoken of *something seen,* viz. of the *sunlight reflected from the ripple of water,* like *smile* and *laugh* in English poetry; as in Hom. Hym. in Cer. 14, γαῖά τε πᾶσ' ἐγέλασσε καὶ ἁλμυρὸν οἶδμα θαλάσσης, where the joyous bright *look* of sea, as well as earth, must be meant.

91. The construction changes in this line. καὶ σέ, ὦ πανόπτα ἡλίου κύκλος, καλῶ, would resemble the form of the preceding clauses.

94. The article is not used with reference to *his* destined term of suffering, but because χρόνος, like monadic appellatives, sometimes takes the article. Comp. τὸν μακρὸν χρόνον, 449, Soph. Œd. Col. 8; τὸν αἰανῆ χρόνον, Furies 542 (572); ὁ μυρίος χρόνος, Soph. Œd. Col. 618; ἐς τοσόνδε τοῦ χρόνου, Soph. Electr. 961. The like is true of βίος with the epithets μακρός, μακραίων, etc., Soph. Œd. Rex 381, 518, and in Soph. Electr. 822, τοῦ βίου δ' οὐδεὶς πόθος, where τοῦ βίου is not *of my life,* but *of life.* —— μυριετῆ is used indefinitely to denote a very long time. Comp. v. 774, where it becomes thirteen generations.

NOTES.   59

99. πῆ depends on στενάχω, as on δέδια, 182, and the clause which it begins is epexegetical of τὸ ἐπερχόμενον πῆμα. —— ἐπιτεῖλαι, *to arise, appear,* = ἀνατεῖλαι. Hesiod (Op. et Dies 384, 565) uses it in the middle, of the rising of the sun and planets.

102. σκεθρῶς, probably from ἔχω, σχεθεῖν, in the sense of *holding on to,* = *closely, accurately.*

109: According to Hesiod (Op. et Dies 52), Prometheus stole fire in the hollow stalk of the *narthex* (or ferula), a tall, umbelliferous plant, used by the worshippers of Bacchus for staves, the dry pith of which kindled easily. The fable in this particular selected a plant used for conveying fire from one neighbour to another, and which is still so employed in Cyprus, under the name of νάρθηκα. (Walpole's Memoirs, 284, in Welcker's Trilogie, 8.)

110. κλοπαίαν does not qualify πηγὴν directly, but denotes the manner in which the action of θηρῶμαι was performed; = κλοπῇ, λάθρα.

112. τοιάσδε. Some MSS. have an easier reading τοιῶνδε, which Brunck and Schütz prefer, because the crime had just been spoken of. But *such a penalty* = a penalty on such grounds.

115. ὀδμά. The poets taught that an ambrosial perfume exhaled from the persons and vestments of the Gods, arising from the fragrant ointments with which they were conceived to anoint themselves after the manner of men. See Iliad xiv. 172. —— ἀφεγγής, *invisible, obscure.* See v. 124, note.

116. κεκραμένη. The Schol. and Schütz take this to mean *pertaining to a demigod,* whose nature is *human and divine mingled.* Others, *pertaining to gods and men both.* This is preferable, since the epithet is used, not of persons but of an odor and a sound.

117. The subject of ἵκετο is implied in the two preceding lines. —— τερμόνιον, *on the borders of the earth.*

121. δι' ἀπεχθείας ἐλθόνθ' = ἐν ἀπεχθείᾳ ὄντα. Comp. Alcest 874.

124. φεῦ expresses wonder here. — v. 115 and this place show that the Chorus were not seen during their approach by Prometheus, and perhaps they came in their car from behind. To the spectator they appear suspended in the air, down to v. 279.

128. φιλία is not an epithet of τάξις, but answers to an adverb in English, = φιλίως. This band came *a friendly one*, i. e. *with kind intent*.

134. θεμερῶπιν, *staid-faced, grave-faced*, from θεμερός, *set, staid, composed*. This word is found in a fragment of the Sicilian comic poet, Epicharmus. Hesychius defines θεμερή by βεβαία, σεμνή, εὐσταθής. The root is (θέω) τίθημι.

135. ἀπέδιλος, sc. owing to their hurry. The ancients put on sandals or slippers when they went out of the house, but were commonly unshod within.

137. πολυτέκνου. Hesiod (Theog. 364) gives three thousand daughters, and as many sons (personified rivers, products of earth and sea), to Oceanus and Tethys.

139. The early Greeks conceived of the earth as land surrounded by water flowing in a perpetual current. Hence Ocean is called a river by Homer, Iliad xviii. 607, and is next to the rim of the shield of Achilles. Herodotus (4. 36) alludes to this opinion, to discard it. The God and the stream are here blended. In vv. 284 and 300 the God is conceived of as coming from the Ocean-stream lying at a great distance to the place where Prometheus is bound, near the northern sea. Comp. v. 581, where the Chorus speaks of sacrifices offered upon the shores of this stream.

144. φοβερά, *ex horrore coorta;* Wellauer. Rather, *fearful, timorous*. The quality is applied to the tears, instead of the person whose fear caused them.

145. εἰσιδοῦσα by a *constructio ad sensum* is referred to ἐμοὶ contained in ἐμοῖσιν ὅσσοις.

147. ταῖς — λύμαις, *in these* (ταῖς is demonstrative) *indignities of iron bonds*, in these injurious chains of iron.

NOTES.

150. ἀθέτως. Schol. ἀνόμως, *arbitrarily*.

151. A Schol. says, πελώρια λέγει καὶ Τιτᾶνας καὶ νόμους αὐτῶν. τὰ πριν πελώρια, *what were heretofore great or mighty*.

153. Tartarus was conceived of as an immense chasm below Hades, or as the lower part of that, the whole of which was called Hades.—ἀπέραντος, *non transcundus;* Blomf. *impenetrabilis, ex quo exire non licet;* Wellauer. *Unlimited*, Passow's Lex.

156, 157. ὡς — ἐπεγήθει, *in order that* (no one) *might have rejoiced.* See vv. 749, 750.

160. ὅτῳ = ὥστε αὐτῷ. Comp. Alcest. 194; Antig. 220.

163. τιθέμενος, a conjectural reading for θέμενος, approved by Hermann and Schütz, and also by Elmsley (who remarks that ἀεὶ is rarely found with the *aorist* particip.), brings the line into measure with v. 182. Porson changed this latter line, and with as much, if not more reason, reading δέδια δ', for δέδια γάρ. τιθέμενος ἄγναμπτον = *rendering, making inflexible*.

167. Comp. vv. 762 *seq*., 908 *seq*.

169. πρύτανις, *chief, head*. So Supplices 366 (371). From πρό. This word was retained in this sense by some Greek states, to denote their chief magistrates : at Athens it meant the sitting committee of the Council.

170. τὸ νέον βούλευμα. Not the plot of another, but his own plan of action, referring to his marriage. Comp. vv. 762, 764.

184. ἀκίχητα, *not to be reached* by prayer, inexorable.

186, 187. τὸ δίκαιον παρ' ἑαυτῷ ἔχων, *keeping justice by himself*, or *within his own power*. Comp. our phrase *to take the law into one's own hands*, and Eurip. Suppl. 431, cited by Blomf., κρατεῖ δ' εἶς, τὸν νόμον κεκτημένος αὐτὸς παρ' αὑτῷ.

193. Take πάντα λόγον together.

201. These nominatives continue the construction of v. 199, and are not nominatives absolute.

202, 203 ἀνάσσῃ, ἄρξειεν. Here the *optative* denotes a merely possible event purposed ; while the *subjunctive* inplies also that it was realized, or that there was a ground for its existence. The *present* denotes continued, the aorist momentary action, in this case that of becoming a ruler. Krüger on Arrian. Anab. II. 3. 6, translates ἄρξαι by *imperio potiri*, and adds, " ita passim βασιλεῦσαι τυραννῆσαι aliique aoristi, quorum præsentia conditionem aliquam significant.' — δῆθεν here, not, as usually, accompanying a false or ironical statement. Comp. 986. — τοὔμπαλιν may be the object of σπεύδοντες. Comp. Electr. 251 ; Plat. Gorg. 455, C.

208. ἀμοχθί. Bl. writes ἀμοχθεί, contending that adverbs from words ending in ος should end in ι, not in ει. Hermann, on Ajax 1206, thinks that such of these adverbs as are derived from verbs should be written with ι, and, as for the rest, " nondum res plane ad liquidum perducta est." With this Buttmann (largest Grammar, 2. 344) substantially agrees.

210. The Scholiasts all take Gæa here for the same person as Themis. But in Furies 2, Æschylus follows the common mythology in making Themis the daughter of Gæa or Earth. The poet means, then, that the grandmother of Prometheus, as well as his mother, foretold to him the future. Gæa is called πρωτόμαντις (*in loc. cit.*) and had many names, as Rhea, Chthon, Demeter. Themis also was prescient (874), and held the oracle at Delphi before Apollo came there. See especially Eurip. Iph. in Tauris 1259, *seq.*

213. χρείη is the optative in *oratione obliqua*. K. § 345. 4. The direct form would be χρή — κρατεῖν. —— τοὺς ὑπερέχοντας, *the victors* (whoever they should be). The participle is used as a noun without respect of time. Several critics, on slight manuscript authority, read ὑπερσχόντας, *those who should get the upper hand.* Blomf. says, " aoristum postulat sensus," I see not why.

215. τὸ πᾶν = πάντως, *wholly, at all.* Comp. Agam. 168 (179).

217. προσλαβόντα, after μοι, construed with the subject of the infinitive, instead of προσλαβόντι, which construction,

though less common, also occurs. Comp. Soph. Electr. 959 – 962, where both are found.

221. αὐτοῖσι συμμάχοισι. The dative, in the relation of accompaniment, is frequently thus used with αὐτός, and for the most part without σύν. Comp. Mt. § 405. 3; K. § 283. 2. (a).

232. ἀϊστώσας is to be taken in translating after ἔχρῃζεν, as if it were· ἔχρῃζεν ἀϊστῶσαι καὶ φιτῦσαι.

235. Most authorities read here ἐξερυσάμην, which is for ἐξερρυσάμην, as ῥύομαι alone, and not ἐρύομαι, is used in the sense *deliver* by the tragic poets. The doubling of ρ is neglected by poetic license, as in χρυσορύτους, Antig. 950. As this is very rare in iambics, ἐξελυσάμην, found in several MSS., is received by Dindorf into his text.

237. τῷ, *propter hoc, igitur.*

239. προθέμενος ἐν οἴκτῳ. Though such phrases as τίθεσθαι ἐν λόγῳ, ἐν αἰσχρῷ, occur, Blomf. says he has not found any similar to the present. It ought to mean, *placing before one's self as objects of pity,* = θέμενος ἐν οἴκτῳ, substantially. The following somewhat analogous expression may be found in Josephus de Bello Jud. III. 10, § 2, τοῦ μὴ δοκεῖν μετὰ τὴν τῆς οἰκουμένης ἡγεμονίαν ἐν ἀντιπάλῳ τὰ Ἰουδαίων προτίθεσθαι, i. e. *to place the Jews before ourselves as rivals.*

241. ὧδ' ἐρρύθμισμαι, "metaphora a verbis desumpta quæ in rhythmum rediguntur et coercentur"; Blomf. = *coerceor, constringor.* Comp. Antig. 318, for the word in another sense.

247. The sense is, *Did you peradventure proceed* any *farther even than this?*

261. καθ' ἡδονὴν = ἡδύ, and is the predicate. Comp. v. 494. —— σοὶ τ' ἄλγος, sc. ἀκούειν, to be supplied by zeugma from λέγειν.

268. For the construction, comp. Alcest. 641, note.

269. κατισχνανεῖσθαι is the fut. mid. inf. used passively (comp. Antig. 210), from κατισχναίνω, *I dry up, make lean.*

κατισχανεῖσθαι is preferred by Porson, on Orest. 292, and Well., and is the reading of all the MSS. except one: the other word answers in sense to προσαναινόμενον, v. 146, and is justly preferred by Blomf. and Dind. ——πεδαρσίοις, Æolic and perhaps older Doric for μεταρσίοις, as πεδαίρειν for μεταίρειν in lyric places of Euripides.

275. ταὐτὰ = κατὰ τὰ αὐτά, *in the same way.* The sense is, *calamity wandering in the same way* (i. e. just as in this case) *now lights on one, now on another.* (Your turn to need sympathy may come.)

279. In the representation the Chorus was now let down from the machine to the stage.

282. πελῶ is future, like σκεδᾷ, v. 25. Comp. v. 303.

284. τέρμα follows ἥκω = ἐπὶ τέρμα. K. § 277.

285. διαμειψάμενος, sc. ὁδόν. Comp. Sept. ad Theb. 316, διαμείψαι δωμάτων στυγερὰν ὁδόν.

287. γνώμῃ, *by my will.* Comp. παρὰ γνώμην, *against my will,* Eurip. Medea 577. Blomf. thinks that this word may denote the *intelligence* of the griffin itself.

289. ξυγγενές. The mythus made Oceanus and Japetus, the father of Prometheus, brothers.

292. The phrase νέμειν μείζονα μοῖραν was occasioned by the custom of setting a greater portion at meals before distinguished persons or strangers. Hence it = *to hold in greater honor.*

301. σιδηρομήτορα. Sometimes compound adjectives in the tragic poets may be resolved into a noun and a genitive depending upon it, sometimes into a noun and its adjective. Thus, σεμνόμαντις, Œd. Rex 556, = σεμνὸς μάντις, and the present word = σιδήρου μήτηρ. Comp. Mt. § 446, Obs. 3, b.

302. ἐς αἶαν, i. e. to Scythia, which was thought to abound in iron.

303. ξυνασχαλῶν is future, like γαμεῖ and ἀσχαλᾷ, v. 764.

309. μεθάρμοσαι — νέους, *change your character into a new one.* νέος shows the result, = ὥστε νέους εἶναι.

NOTES.

313. χόλον — μόχθων, *gall* or *bitterness of sufferings.*

317 ἀρχαῖα, *antiquated, exploded, foolish.* For the form of this sentence, comp. Alcest. 256.

319. ἐπίχειρα. Comp. Antig. 820.

323. This same figure is used Agam. 1607, πρὸς κέντρα μὴ λάκτιζε, by other profane writers, and in Acts xxvi. 15.

328. περισσόφρων, *sapiens plus quam satis est,* Blomf. = *overwise; valde intelligens,* Well. The latter meaning is more apposite, as the word is used to give a reason why he should perceive the force of the remark.

329. προστρίβεται, *is rubbed upon,* as dirt upon cloth, *is inflicted.*

330. κυρεῖς = κυρεῖς ὤν. K. § 310, R. 5. Comp. Electr. 313; Antig. 487. The participle is often suppressed.

331. καὶ τετολμηκὼς ἐμοί. ἐμοὶ is to be taken with both participles, and the notion of companionship is carried over from μετασχών, so that τετολ. is briefly for συντετολ.

332. μηδὲ μελησάτω. The *second* person imperative of the aorist is rarely used with the negative, but instead of it, the subjunctive; the *third* person so used is more common. Comp. Alcest. 1077; Mt. § 511. 3; K. § 259. 5, R. 9.

335. τοὺς πέλας, *others, another.* See Antig. 479, and Electra 551, note (second edition). — φρενοῦν limits ἀμείνων, which, like *better,* has the sense of *better able.* Comp. Persæ 676, "the gods below" λαβεῖν ἀμείνους εἰσὶν ἢ μεθιέναι.

336. ἔργῳ — λόγῳ here *by matter of fact which I see, not by what is told to me.* The words are very often contrasted in somewhat different shades of meaning.

338. αὐχῶ. Comp. Alcest. 95; Antig. 390.

340. τὰ μέν σ' = τὰ μέν σε, τὰ μὲν being opposed to ἀτάρ. Others read τὰ μὲν σ', i. e. σά. —— λήξω, sc. ἐπαινῶν.

341. προθυμίας is governed by ἐλλείπεις.

347. The passage from this line to 372, Elmsley first gave to Prometheus, all the MSS. and preceding editors having assigned it to Oceanus. Blomf., Well, and others, follow

Elmsley's conjecture, which is, I think, clearly correct. οἰ δῆτα reaffirms what Prometheus had said, and introduces an instance of his sympathy; but, in the mouth of Oceanus, it is not at all to the point. That *he* felt sympathy was no reason to suppose that Prometheus, in his very different situation, should feel it also. The prophecy, again, in v. 367, comes most appropriately from the mouth of the son of Themis. V. 373 not only cannot begin a new discourse without great abruptness, but it necessarily continues the preceding discourse, which contains an argument to Oceanus not to oppose Zeus. The words οὐδ' ἐμοῦ διδασκάλου χρῄζεις will have no pertinence, if Prometheus has not been teaching his friend what the cost is of disobedience to the supreme ruler. It may be added that Atlas was the brother, not of Oceanus, but of Prometheus (the sons of Japetus in Hesiod — Theog. 510 — being Prometheus, Epimetheus, Atlas, and Menœtius); and that κασιγνήτου must be *my brother*. For a conjecture as to the origin of this passage, see the Preface.

351. Æschylus seems, in this extended description of Typhon, to have had Pindar's first Pythian before his eyes, which was written but a little before the Prometheus: indeed, the imitation is close, but it falls far short of the original, which is one of the brightest gems in Greek poetry. It may even be justly charged with being turgid. — γηγενῆ. In Hesiod's Theogony this Typhon or Typhoeus is the youngest child of Gæa, born in Tartarus. He is subterranean fire personified; the cause of volcanic eruptions and earthquakes.

352. δάϊον, *wretched*. In this sense the Doric form is used by the tragic poets; but in the sense *hostile*, δήϊος. So Hermann on Ajax 771.

353. In this line, I follow Porson and Schütz in reading ἑκατογκάρηνον. Blomf. and Elmsley prefer, as more Attic, ἑκατογκάρανον. The reading of the MSS., ἑκατοντακάρηνον,

violates the metre, by giving an anapæst in the second place; but is still retained by Well., who thinks that the poet designedly departed from the rule, in order, by an additional syllable, to express more vastness.

354. This line in the MSS., with the reading πᾶσιν δς ἀντέστη θεοῖς, contains an inadmissible anapæst in the fourth place, which many critics have tried to do away with. Wunderlich proposed ἀνέστη, and supposed the construction to be ὃς ἀνέστη συρίζων φόνον πᾶσι θεοῖς. Dindorf (Præf. ad Poet. Scen.) removes every difficulty by adopting this reading, and taking ἀνέστη θεοῖς together, in the sense, *rose up against the gods*. He cites for this use Iliad xxiii. 635:

Ἀγκαῖον δὲ (ἐνίκησα) πάλῃ Πλευρώνιον, ὅς μοι ἀνέστη.

The relation of the dative here is the same as with μάχομαι, and other verbs of fighting.

355, 356. γαμφηλαῖς Hesych. defines by σιαγόσι, *jawbones, jaws*. —— ἀστράπτω is not often used actively, as here.

358. ἦλθεν αὐτῷ = ἦλθε πρὸς αὐτόν. Comp. Antig. 234.

360. Comp. v. 134, where the *thing*, here the genitive, is the accusative, and the reverse is true of the *person*. —— For φρένας of the next line, comp. v. 881.

362. ἐκβροντᾶν σθένος, *to take away the strength by a stroke of thunder*, — in the passive, *to have one's strength so taken away*. The accusative, standing as the object of the active in Greek, is often joined to the passive to define its action, instead of being its subject; thus, ἀποτέμνειν τὴν κεφαλήν, *to cut the head off;* ἀποτμηθέντες τὰς κεφαλάς, *having had their heads cut off*, Xen. Anab. II. 6. 1. All such cases may be resolved into ἔχω, with the participle of the verb used, and the accus. Sometimes a dative is used instead of an accus. in such phrases. Thus, ἐξηρτημένοι τόξοις, v. 711, means *having bows hanging from them*, lit. *hung with bows*. Comp. Soph. Electra 54.

366. μυδροκτυπεῖ. Comp. Soph. Antig. 264.

368. γνάθοις. For this word used metaphorically, comp. vv. 64, 726. — For the allusion here, see the Preface.

369. λευράς, *broad, spacious,* an Homeric word, used Odys. vii. 123. Comp. v. 394, where it has the same sense.

371. θερμοῖς — ζάλης, literally *through the hot darts of his insatiate fire-breathing fury,* i. e. by means of the hot eruptions of an incessant storm of fire.

378. ὀργή, *feelings, temper,* = ψυχή, which appears in citations of this verse. Cicero, however, in his translation of this verse renders it by *iracundiæ,* and θυμὸν can take this sense also.

380. The sense is, *and not try to reduce swelling anger by force.* ἰσχναίνω, *I make thin,* or *lean.* " Ducta est," says Schütz, " elegans allegoria e medicorum rationibus, qui corporis tumori fomenta adhibent." Comp. v. 269.

381. προμηθεῖσθαι, which alludes to the name of Prometheus, is preferred by Brunck, Valckenaer, Porson, Blomf., and Dind. to προθυμεῖσθαι, a reading of more MS. authority; but must be merely an emendation of a bad reading προμυθεῖσθαι. προθυμεῖσθαι expresses the forwardness to serve a friend, which Oceanus professed, as the ensuing lines show. Comp. also v. 341.

385. A Scholiast paraphrases this line thus : — " It is better for me while I have good designs and useful for you to pass with most persons as void of understanding." He takes εὖ φρονεῖν in the moral sense, and so G. Schneider. It must, I think, have the intellectual sense : *It is best where one is wise not to pass for such,* i. e. " that is far better than like you to pass for a wise person, and thereby expose one's self to Jupiter's tyrannical dislike of every thing great."

386. τόδε τὸ ἀμπλάκημα means the error in such a course as Oceanus advocates, i. e. in attempting to soften the tyrant's will. The proud soul of Prometheus cannot bear to seem to have used Oceanus as an unsuccessful mediator with Jove.

388. οὑμὸς θρῆνος. Comp. Alcest. 336.

389. Verbs of *sitting* in the poets sometimes are followed

by the accusative of the *seat*. Comp. Œd. Rex 2. This is analogous to such phrases as *to walk the earth, to swim the sea.*

394. ψαίρει. Griffiths shows that this word answers to our *flap*. It here denotes the gentle movements of the animal's wings in preparation for flight.

397. For the construction of στένω, see Alcest. 652.

399. Most editors omit λειβομένα without MS. authority, and with one MS. read ἔτεγξε, thus producing equality between the strophe and antistrophe ; but the latter shows marks of a lacuna. The measure is injured by δ' after δακρυσίστακτον. —— ῥαδινῶν, *soft, tender*. The general idea of this word is *ease* of motion, which appears in the senses *pliant, nimble, graceful,* and, by consequence, *slender* (connected with *graceful*, as a thick-set frame is opposed to grace), and *tender* or *soft*, as pliant twigs are. There is very good authority for ῥαδινόν. —— ῥέος = ῥεῦμα. —— λειβομένα. For the middle of λείβω, comp. Alcest. 1015.

401. παγαῖς. Richmond remarks that πηγὴ denotes not only a *spring*, but *water flowing from a spring*, a stream. This is the case here, and in v. 434.

402. Well. puts a point after τάδε, and writes Ζεὺς δ'. "Utrumque," says he, "sensus requirit, et recepi ex Robortello, præeunte Hermanno." But δέ produces an unpleasant contrast between the clauses, and a point after τάδε brings too much abruptness into the style. ἀμέγαρτα τάδε = ἀμεγάρτως οὕτως, λυγρῶς οὕτως, *thus unenviably, thus grievously*. Comp. Buttmann's Lexil., No. 61, for this word.

405. αἰχμή, *sceptre*, thence *power ;* " *vis*, proprie *hasta*, quam reges antiquos pro sceptro gestasse monet Butlerus " ; Blomf. Comp. v. 925.

406. στονόεν = στονοέντως.

409. Four syllables are wanting before στένουσα. Many editors read στένουσι, which has no subject, unless it be implied in χώρα. The line is also corrupt, as the τ' between

the first and third words shows. —— ἀρχαιοπρεπῆ, *illustrious of old*. Comp. ἀρχαιόπλουτος, *rich of old*, Agam. 1013 (1043). —— στένειν τιμὴν here means, to lament *the loss* of honor, but σ. συμφοράν, somewhere else, to lament *the existence* of misfortune. Something so, ὑπηρετεῖν νόσῳ, Soph. Œd. Rex 217, to aid in *removing* a disease; but ὑπηρετεῖν λόγῳ, Eurip. Medea 588 (Porson), to aid in *carrying forward* a plan.

410. ξυνομαιμόνων. The Titans in general, and not simply the brothers of Prometheus. So Scholefield.

411. ἔποικον, Blomf., Schütz, Passow, *neighbouring*; Wellauer, *inhabited*. —— ἁγνᾶς, *sacred*, sc. as being personified and an object of worship.

416. μάχας in the genitive. Comp. Mt. § 339.

420. Why is Arabia mentioned here, while all the other places are near the Euxine? Some suppose the text to be wrong, which is not unlikely. Others say Arabia was taken in a wide sense: but it could never include the vicinity of Caucasus. "Verisimile est," says Elmsley, " Æschylum geographiæ nihilo peritiorem fuisse Tragico nostrati, (Shakspeare in the 'Winter's Tale,') qui oram Bohemiæ maritimam memorat."

421. ὑψίκρημνον, *on a high crag*. It is uncertain what city is here meant.

424. ὀξυπρώροισι, *sharp-pointed*. πρώρα is the forward extremity, the front, of any thing; and the front of a spear directed against a foe is its point. καλλίπρωρος in Sept. ad Theb. 515 (533) means *fair-faced*.

425. The sense here is, *one other Titan only have I seen heretofore in calamities, subdued by disgraceful bonds of steel,— the God Atlas*. The other Titans were not so chained, but shut up in Tartarus out of sight.

428–430. ὑπέροχον σθένος. "Subaudiendum videtur κατά." Blomf. That is, *as to* or *with his surpassing might*. A Schol., taking σθένος to mean *weight*, paraphrases the place thus: ὅστις διόλου βαστάζει ὑπείροχον καὶ μέγα βάρος, τὸν κραταιὸν οὐράνιόν τε κύκλον. Some violently put γάϊον in the place of κραταιόν, thereby intruding, as I believe, upon Æschylus the conception that Atlas supported earth as well as heaven. The passage is without doubt corrupt, and has never been cleared from difficulties. σθένος, which can only be in the accusative, cannot mean *weight;* and κραταιόν, whether joined to it or to πολόν, is extremely flat, and must have stolen into the place of some participle or verb expressing the straining of the strength of Atlas. For ὑποστενάζει, which, as involving the notion of *holding up*, is taken in a *constructio prægnans* with νώτοις, Hermann conjectured (Opusc. 1. 114) ὑποστεγάζει, *sustains from underneath*, a rare, if not unknown, word of convenient signification, which derives support from the epithet οὐρανοστεγῆ, *heaven-sustaining*, found in a frag. of Æschylus (No. 285 Dindorf) where Atlas is spoken of. Other emendations and constructions are still less satisfactory than those already given.

431. κλύδων seems to be collective = *surges:* hence the use of ξυμπιτνῶν, *dashing together*. So κῦμα is used by Herodot. 7. 193.

433. Ἄϊδος (from Ἄϊς = Ἀΐδης) depends on μυχὸς γᾶς, and γᾶς on μυχὸς simply. Render, *the cavern of the earth belonging to Pluto*, i. e. Pluto's underground cavern.

438. προυσελούμενον = ὑβριζόμενον. The Etymologicon Magnum, under προσέληνοι, says, προυσελεῖν λέγουσι τὸ ὑβρίζειν. προυσελοῦμεν occurs Aristoph. Frogs 730, according to the best MS., the only other place where this word is found out of Hesychius. See Buttmann's Lexilogus, No. 89, for an essay upon this word.

450. ἔφυρον, *mixed up, confused*, did in confusion and without system. — For οὐ following οὔτε in the next line, a negligence not uncommon, comp. Mt. § 609; K. § 321. 2, Rem. 6; and v. 480. See also Antig. 250, 258.

452. ἄησυροι. This word is elsewhere found in no earlier

author than Apol. Rhod. ii. 1102, cited by Blomf., where it is spoken of the wind, and answers, according to the Schol., to ἐλαφρῶς πνέων. Suidas quotes ἄησυρον κάμψει γόνυ, where it means *light, agile*. It is explained in the scholia and lexicons by κοῦφον, ἐλαφρόν, λεπτόν. Its meanings arranged in order may have been *easily blown by the wind, light*, thence *agile, small*, as light bodies or animals usually are.

454. Here we have an early Greek division of the year into three parts; χεῖμα, *rainy time* (χέω), ἔαρ, *early season*, θέρος, *hot* or *dry time*. From θέρος, ὀπώρα, *late season* (end of summer), and φθινόπωρον, *late autumn*, were taken off, and other subdivisions still were made.

457. The celestial phenomena which fell from age to age upon nearly the same day of the year were used to mark the seasons. Thus in Hesiod (Op. et Dies 383) the heliacal rising of the Pleiades begins the time of harvest (answering to our 11th of May), and their cosmical setting ($=$ October 26) the time of ploughing, or winter. The acronycal rising of Arcturus (its rising at sunset) marked the commencement of spring (ibid. 564).

459. ἀριθμόν, *number, the art of number.*

461. μνήμην, not mnemonics, which was not an old art, but *the power of remembering* gained by practice, which, where books were rare, was a power much exercised. The poet here alludes to the mythus, which made Mnemosyne or Memory mother of the Muse, i. e. of the inventive power of the mind displayed in the arts; for μοῦσα, Dor. μῶσα, feminine participle of μάω, is nothing more than the inventive or investigating one,—personified invention. μουσομήτωρ, then, is *mother of invention*, or *of the arts, inventive*.

463. ζεύγλη was the collar at each end of the ζυγὸν in which the neck of the animal was inserted.

464. For the construction of διάδοχος, comp. Alcest. 655.

465. γένωνθ'. The elision of αι in verbal endings is rare in the tragic poets. See my note on Electr. 818. To avoid

this elision many edd. read γένοινθ' without MS. authority The subjunctive is here used on account of the enduring consequences in the present time.

472. υἰκὲς for ἀεικές. Comp. αἰκία, ἄκων, αἴρω, ἀργός, for ἀεικία, ἀέκων, ἀείρω, ἀεργός.

474. σεαυτὸν properly belongs to the second clause, as its subject, being attracted into the first, as if it were ὁποίοις φαρμάκοις εἰ αὐτὸς ἰάσιμος. K. § 347, Rem. 3. Comp. Plato Charmid. 164, B, ἐνίοτε ὁ ἰατρὸς οὐ γιγνώσκει ἑαυτὸν ὡς ἔπραξε.

480. Nearly all the MSS. have οὐδὲ — οὐ — οὐδέ, which is not good Greek. The words βρώσιμον, χριστόν, πιστόν, belong to the class ἀλέξημα; but the force of οὐδὲ would be to separate them from it, as being distinct classes of themselves. When a *whole* is denied by οὐ, οὐδέ, or οὐδέν, the parts are denied by οὔτε — οὔτε, and οὐ is used for οὔτε, as in v. 451. ———— πιστὸν is the verbal of πιπίσκω, *bibere facio*.

486. κληδών, *an omen from words or sounds casually uttered*; σύμβολος, *a sign from something casually met*. ———— ὕπαρ, i. e. καθ' ὕπαρ, *when we are awake*.

490–492. A reading εὐώνυμοι preferred by Brunck, Schütz, Blomf., and Elmsley, is more grammatical than εὐωνύμους, which most MSS., Well., and Dind. have; but for that very reason looks like an emendation. εὐωνύμους stands, by a familiar change of construction, for εὐώνυμοι, διώρισα being supplied in thought. εὐώνυμος is a euphemistic word for ἀριστερός, *left, sinister*. See Electr. 19, note. Two lines below, the construction changes after ἔχουσι: instead of ἔχθρας — συνεδρίας, governed by ἔχουσι, we have nominatives with εἰσὶ understood; and again in v. 493, the former construction with διώρισα is returned to. ———— συνεδρίαι, the *alighting together of different kinds of birds*.

494. Comp. καθ' ἡδονήν, v. 261.

495. λοβός, the *lobe* or *flap of the liver*.

498, 499. φλογωπὰ σήματα, *signs by flame*: comp. Antig. 1005 *seq.*, i. e. by the burning of victims. —— ἐξωμμάτωσα, properly *I gave sight to*; figuratively, *I rendered clear.* —— ἐπάργεμα, *covered with the albugo*, or white upon the iris, thence *obscure.* Comp. Agam. 1084 (1113), Choëph. 654 (665). — For the whole passage, comp. Antig. 1005 *seq.*

506. The allegorical meaning of the fable of Prometheus seems to have been present to the poet's mind in this passage, from v. 439. As Prometheus is the speaker, of course a very favorable account is given of his interference in favor of mankind. The earliest version of this fable may be found in Hesiod's Works and Days. There is another differing from this in Hesiod's Theogony. In the fable, Prometheus, as the name shows, is understanding or forethought personified, as his brother Epimetheus is afterthought, thought after action or imprudence. He steals fire from heaven for men, and thus represents the human mind reaching after knowledge above its condition, in order that men "may be as Gods, knowing good and evil." Man in the fable is punished by means of Pandora, the woman whom he received; who perhaps stands for sensuality, and who opened the way for all the woes of the race. Prometheus is punished by the vulture of restless, unsatisfied desire gnawing his heart, and by the chains of earthly impotence, which gall his free will and aspiring thoughts; until, by the consent of Jupiter, Hercules slays the vulture and looses the bonds; and a God (see v. 1027) bears the penalty in his place. He now becomes reconciled to the sway of Jove. That there is in this fable — if we overlook some unessential circumstances — a striking resemblance to the Scriptural account of the fall of man cannot be doubted; though it may be hard to say whether the fable grew up on Greek ground, or was an altered form of an old tradition. But what shall we say of the interposition of Jupiter's son, and

of the pains borne by Chiron for Prometheus, which are strangely like the last and greatest truth of revelation? How can we think that heathen fables knew aught of what was but darkly seen even by Jewish prophets?

508. ἀκήδει *take no care* of: a rare word, found twice in Homer, Iliad xiv. 427, xxiii. 70.

516. The Fates ordain; the Furies execute, especially when murders have been committed. The extent of authority here given to the Furies is remarkable. In this play the Fates are placed above Jupiter (515 – 517, 769, 771, 918 *seq.*), but in other pieces of Æschylus are subordinate to him, or united in idea with him, as the highest power. Even here his own free act (performed, however, in ignorance of its consequences) will bring about what is fated. " The poet modifies the relation between him and them according to the nature of the subject. Prometheus belongs to the purely mythic period; and Æschylus could therefore follow the idea which might be formed concerning Jupiter soon after he had dethroned his father." Blümner on the Idea of Destiny, p. 122, in the German.

521. ἦ πού. Comp. Alcest. 199. —— σεμνόν, *solemn, awful.*

525. The sense is, *By no means may Jupiter, who sways all things, set his might in opposition to my will.*

530. θοίναις, *sacrificial feasts*, those, perhaps, which the Æthiopians (Iliad i. 423) made.

535. The metaphor in ἐμμένοι, ἐκτακείη, is drawn from something soft, as wax, melted into or upon any thing. In Electra 1311, Sophocles has the expression μῖσος ἐντέτηκέ μοι, *hatred is melted into me;* and in Trach. 463, ἐντακῆναι τῷ φιλεῖν, *to be melted into love*, i. e. to cleave to it.

537. τείνειν βίον is not *to prolong life*, but simply *to live on, to live.* Life is conceived of as a space continually extending onward in length.

545. " Constructio est," says Blomf., " φέρ' εἰπέ, ὅπως

ἄχαρις χάρις." It is better to follow the Scholiast, who paraphrases this passage thus: φέρε, ὦ φίλος, ἐπειδή, ἣν εἰς τοὺς βροτοὺς πεποίηκας χάριν, ἄχαρις (ἐστί). ὅπως = as, since. —— ἄχαρις χάρις, *a thankless favor.* Comp. Antig. 1261, and ἄχαρις χάρις, 904 infra, where see the note. —— ποῦ τίς ἀλκά ; " dupliciter interrogatur." Reisig.

555, &c. The sense is, *This song, which has come into my mind, is of opposite import from that, when I sung hymeneal hymns around thy bath and marriage-bed.* The Greeks said either τοῦτο διαφέρει τούτου, or τοῦτο καὶ τοῦτο διαφέρουσι, or τοῦτο διαφέρει καὶ τοῦτο. This last is the form of the present sentence. The poet might have said τόδε τὸ μέλος προσέπτα διαμφίδιον, making δ. the predicate; instead of which he employs it as an epithet, and brings in τόδε afterwards, as epexegetical of μέλος. —— διαμφίδιον, Hesych. ἀλλοῖον, διὰ παντὸς κεχωρισμένον, a word only found here, from διαμφίς, *wide apart.* —— ὅτε. Some authorities have ὅ τε, from ὅς τε, but there is no evidence that the rare word ὑμεναιόω (which = ᾄδω τὸν ὑμέναιον) can be taken actively. —— προσέπτα. The figure in this word denotes the approach of something inperceptible or immaterial, moving lightly or suddenly. Comp. vv. 115, 644. —— ἀμφὶ λουτρά. Bathing took place among the preparative ceremonies of marriage. Comp. Eurip. Phœniss. 347. —— ἰότατι = ἕνεκα. —— τὰν ὁμοπάτριον, *sprung from the same father* with us. Hesione was a daughter of Oceanus and Tethys, according to Acusilaus, one of the earliest prose genealogists, in Buttmann's Scholia on the Odyssey, x. 2. —— ἕδνοις. The construction here is, as Schütz remarks, Ἡσιόνην ἕδνοις πιθὼν ἤγαγες δάμαρτα.

561. The mythus of Io seems originally to have had a physical meaning. Io is the moon (the *traveller,* Ἰὼ from εἶμι, as Ὑπερίων, the sun, denotes the traveller on high), and Argus, with innumerable eyes, is the starry sky by night. He is the perpetual companion of Io, until Hermes, the

bringer on of night and day, destroys him, i. e. restores the daylight. The horns of the moon led many tribes to conceive of their moon-goddess as a heifer, and such is Io's form. Having become a mythological person, she came into the poet's region, and was brought into connection with other fictions. She ceased, perhaps, to be a goddess of high rank, when the worship of another tribe was brought to Argos.

564. ποινὰς ὀλέκει. ποινάς, ποινᾶς, ποινῆς, ποινή σ', occur as various readings. The position of these forms represents the progress from truth to a conjecture through a false reading. The accusative ποινὰς is put in a sort of apposition with the verb. Comp. Mt. § 432; K. § 266, Rem. 2. The sense is, *In penalty for what crime you are perishing?*

567. οἶστρος. There is no reason to suppose that any thing was presented to the eyes of the spectators; but still the poet plainly uses this word literally: Io thought of the spectre of Argus, as a real œstrus buzzing arround her, as is shown by v. 675. —— In this line τὰν was first inserted by Hermann, then by Elmsley and others. In the next ἄλευ δᾶ is Dindorf's reading for ἄλευ' ὢ δᾶ. See the Pref. to his " Poetæ Scenici," p. vi.

568. γηγενοῦς. Like Typhon, the Cyclopes, the Titans, and other monsters, Argus is here said to be earth-born, or the son of Gæa. His parentage is variously given, but Acusilaus calls him Gæa's son in Apollodor. II. 1. 3.

569. Two Vienna MSS. omit φοβοῦμαι, and two others read εἰσορῶ. Both seem, according to Dindorf, to be additions to the text, εἰσορῶσα having originally stood alone without a verb, the idea, *I fear*, being implied in the context. Comp. Matthiæ on Hecuba 950 (971), αἰδώς μ' ἔχει — τυγχάνουσα, for αἰδοῦμαι — τυγχάνουσα. I have inserted φοβοῦμαι in the text in brackets, though disposed to assent to Dindorf's correction.

574. ὑπὸ δὲ κ. τ. λ. The sense is, *And his sonorous wax-joined reed sounds forth in an undertone a sleep-giving lay*

—— By δόναξ is intended the syrinx or Pan's pipe of reeds of different lengths cemented together.

575. ὑπνοδόταν. This word, perhaps, is used to set forth the torment of Io, inclined to sleep, but still driven forward by the œstrus.

576. For τηλέπλανοι πλάναι, comp. vv. 585, 900.

577. Join τί ποτε ἁμαρτοῦσαν εὑρών together, = *having found me in what sin.*

580. οἰστρηλάτῳ δείματι, *the fear caused by the pursuing œstrus.*

584. φθονέω, like μεγαίρω, v. 626, governs the genitive of the thing grudged or denied. Comp. Mt. § 368, a ; K. § 274.

588. This verse was first made part of Io's song by Hermann and Elmsley, instead of being ascribed to the Chorus. This is necessary according to the usual practice of the tragic poets, if the corresponding verse in the antistrophe belongs to her.

592. στυγητός. It is rare that verbals in τός have but two endings. γνωτός is so used Œd. Rex 396. Comp. Alcest. 102, note. —— γυμνάζομαι denotes *to practise with effort or pain, to use strength, or labor upon*, and takes an accusative, as τέχνην. Plat. Gorg. 514, E.

594. τίς — προσθροεῖς, *who art thou, who, I say, that addressest me thus correctly?* For the condensed form of the sentence (= τίς εἶ — ὃς προσθροεῖς), comp. Alcest. 106 note.

599. φοιταλέοις, ὁρμητικοῖς, Schol. ; *circumagentibus*, Well Rather, *maddening.*

600. σκιρτημάτων αἰκίαις, i. e. *tormenting leaps.* The œstrus drove her forward in a painful race, allowing her no time for food.

601. Ἥρας. This word is due to a conjecture of Hermann, and appears in the modern edd. Such a dissyllabic word was wanting to complete the metre, and the Scholiasts introduce it in paraphrasing ἐπικότοισι μήδεσι.

606. For τί μὴ χρή, Elmsley elegantly conjectured τί μῆ-χαρ, *what cure*, and put a point after παθεῖν. This, with ἣ following it, which is Reisig's emendation, I have received into this third edition.

612. βροτοῖς, as well as πυρὸς, depends on δοτῆρα. Comp. Mt. § 389. 3.

615. ἁρμοῖ = ἀρτίως. Properly it is an old dative, — like οἴκοι, πεδοῖ, — from ἁρμός, *joint*. The time denoted by *just now* is a time *joined on, adjoining* to the present. Comp. *juxta* from *jungo*.

617. For μου some authorities for the text read μοι. A similar dative sometimes follows δέχομαι.

621. ἀρκῶ σαφηνίσαι = ἀρκεῖ ἐμὲ σαφηνίσαι. Comp. Antig. 547.

626. See 584.

627. μὴ οὐ. Comp. Mt. § 609; K. § 318. 10. τί μέλλεις being in fact negative = μὴ μελλε, this case of μὴ οὐ is like that in vv. 796, 918.

628. θράττω is an Attic form for ταράττω. Comp. φροίμιον for προοίμιον. See Buttmann, Lexil., No. 52. 3.

629. The sense demanded by the context is that of μᾶσσον (= μᾶλλον) ἢ ὡς, which is the reading of two or three MSS.; ἢ ὡς being pronounced as one syllable. Several scholars, as Dindorf on this passage, Kühner (largest Gram., § 748. 2) and Bremi on Lysias (ed. Gotha, 1826, p. 46), after Herm. on Viger, contend that ὡς can follow the comparative in the sense of ἤ. Blomf. agrees with the Scholiasts in giving to ὡς the sense of ὅτι, *nam, siquidem*, and understanding ἀκοῦσαι with γλυκύ. Griffiths renders ὡς *how*. *Be no longer anxious how it may please me.* Both of these explanations fail to satisfy, nor is Elmsley's conjecture μασσόνως ἢ 'μοι γλυκὺ to be commended.

636. The river-god, Inachus, was born of Oceanus, like the ocean-nymphs, or Oceanides, who compose the Chorus.

638. οἴσεσθαι. φέρομαι in the middle often means *I bear off, obtain* as a prize.

639. ἀξίαν τριβὴν ἔχει, *are a proper way of spending time, are well worth while.*

645. πολεύμεναι for πολούμεναι = the Homeric πωλεύμεναι, which is perhaps the true reading. Comp. Alcest. 29, for this word.

648. δαρόν, Dor. for δηρόν, is used in iambics by Æsch. and Eurip.

650. ξυναίρεσθαι, *take upon him together with you, join you in.*

652. βαθύν, *having a deep soil, fertile.* Comp. νειὸς βαθεῖα, Hom.

654. τὸ δῖον ὄμμα = τὸ Διὸς ὄμμα. Comp. Alcest. 5.

655. εὐφρόνας. See Electra 19.

658. ἐπὶ Δωδώνης. The genitive with ἐπὶ often follows a verb of motion, in answer to the question whither.

659. The majority of the MSS. read μάθῃ, with which ἐρῆ in its time accords.

660. Comp. v. 494, and Soph. Œd. Rex 72.

666. ἄφετον ἀλᾶσθαι. There is an allusion here to sacred cattle, which were called ἄφετοι and ἄνετοι, as being left free to wander where they chose, a custom still prevailing in India. See the notes on Hesychius, *voce* ἄφετοι.

667. μολεῖν. Here the aorist infin. stands after βάξις ἦλθεν, with a future sense; even though that phrase has no future idea, such as verbs of hoping, promising, and the like have, with which aor. infinitives are often so used. Comp. Mt. § 501. The more regular form of this sentence would be εἰ μὴ θέλοι — μολεῖν ἂν — ὃς ἐξαιστώσοι. μολεῖν, for the fut. μολεῖσθαι, and ἐξαιστώσοι, take the form which belongs to *oratio directa*, thus by a change of construction deserting the optative. An obvious conjecture of Elmsley's, πυρωπὸν ἂν for π. ἐκ, is then unnecessary.

676. Κερχνείας. Another reading is Κεγχρείας. So its primitive has the forms κέρχνον, κέγχρον, *millet.* I do not find a stream of this name elsewhere mentioned as being in

Argolis. It may have been one of the little water-courses running towards Lerna, not far from the village of Cenchreæ, which lay on the road from Tegea to Argos.

677. ἄκρην. This reading is probably corrupt, as the discrepancies of the MSS. seem to show. "Nusquam, quod sciam, memoratur Λέρνης ἄκρα." Blomf. Dindorf justly approves of the conjecture Λέρνης τε κρήνην, which Blomf. has admitted into his text. The Scholiast, by his gloss πρὸς τὴν Λέρνην τὴν πηγήν, shows that this was in his copy. Lerna was a morass on a low coast from which the hills retired.

680. ἀπροσδόκητος = ἀπροσδοκήτως. —— The last two syllables of αἰφνίδιος are probably pronounced as one by synizesis. For the synizesis of ι, which Porson denied, see Herm. Elementa, p. 34, ed. Glasg. Elmsley removed the necessity for it by proposing to read ἀφνίδιος.

682. γῆν πρὸ γῆς, *to land in front of*, i. e. *beyond land.* Not so Mt. § 575.

683. κλύεις. The present of this verb and of ἀκούω and πυνθάνομαι, like "hear," "learn," in English, is used in speaking of past time, both when, as here, the thing heard is so recently spoken of, that the sound is, so to speak, still in the ears; and also when a rumor or report lasting until the present time is referred to. Thus one can say at the close of a speech or story, "you hear the argument," or "narrative," (= it is in your ears,) and we say, "I hear that the steamboat is arrived " (= λέγεται, it is said, such is the report).

698. τοι. Comp. v. 39.

700. τὴν πρὶν χρείαν ἠνύσασθε, *you fulfilled your former desire.*

711. ἐξηρτημένοι τόξοις. Comp. 362. Scholefield cites Hor. Epist., Lib. I. 1. 56, "Lævo suspensi loculos tabulamque lacerto." One MS. has the easier reading ἐξηρτυμένοι, *furnished with.* —— The Scythians, and some of the Sarmatæ, led a nomad life, and had no fixed mansions, but dwel

in wagons, whence one tribe of Scythians derived the name of Hamaxobii. Comp. Herod. 4. 46; Strabo 7. 3, § 2. The Tartars have still this same kind of houses on wheels. William de Rubruquis saw them in the year 1253, and describes them thus (Transl. in Pinkerton, Vol. VII. p. 28): —" Their houses they raise upon a round foundation of wickers artificially wrought and compacted together; the roof consisting of wickers also, meeting above in one little roundel, out of which there rises upward a neck like a chimney, which they cover with white felt, &c. — These houses they made so large that they contain thirty feet in breadth; — I told two-and-twenty oxen in one draught drawing a house upon a cart." And so Marco Polo (Pinkerton, Vol. VII. p. 123).

712, &c. What is said by the poet concerning Io's wanderings is quite at variance with geographical truth, and it is difficult to say in all cases what view of her course he had in his own mind. From the vicinity of Argos (676) she went to the oracle of Dodona (830), and to the coast of the Ionian or Adriatic Sea. Thence she turned, travelling no longer in a westerly direction; but the poet is silent about her path, until she arrives at the scene of this play, which seems to have been the shore of the Hyperborean or Scythian Sea. This sea Æschylus may have regarded as being far to the south of its actual place. Io now goes towards the east (707), and avoids the Scythian nomads by drawing nigh to a rocky coast, which Schütz takes for that of the Palus Mæotis. The Chalybes are an otherwise unknown nation of that name, so called from their skill in working iron. A number of barbarous tribes, both in mythic and in historic geography, bore this appellation. Xenophon fell in with two; one near Armenia (Anab. IV. 5. 34), and another not far from Trapezus (*ibid.*, V. 5. 1). The Hybristes is explained to be the Araxes by the Scholiasts; their ground may have been, that both names denote the violence of the current. Schütz, however, takes this river to be the Tanais, which was falsely supposed by some, according to Strabo, to run north from Caucasus. —— πελάζειν, with dative, K. § 284. 2.

713. A single ρ following the syllable on which the ictus is laid can make it long, but the short syllable in *thesis* after ρ is still short, as here. Comp. vv. 992 and 1023.

714. λαιᾶς χειρός, Mt. § 377. This local genitive is rare even in the poets.

718. εὔβατος περᾶν. See v. 766.

719. πρὸς αὐτὸν K., *to Caucasus itself*, as contrasted with the river flowing from it, = *quite to Caucasus*. Others explain αὐτὸν K. as meaning *Caucasus properly so called*, i. e. the main or highest part of the mountain. But there is nothing said in the context of any other part of the mountain, which can be set in contrast to the highest part.

725 – 728. ἵνα, *where*. If the text is right, the geography is exceedingly wrong. The mouth of the Thermodon, on the southern coast of the Euxine, was some ten degrees of longitude east of Salmydessus on the western. Of this the poet could hardly be ignorant, as the Euxine trade of Athens must already have become considerable. He may, however, have followed some of the early fables relating to the Argonauts, in placing this town on the southern coast. To avoid the difficulty here noticed, Völcker, in his Mythische Geographie, begins a new sentence at ἵνα, while G. Schneider joins ἵνα, not with the clause before it, but with βῆναι. In the latter case, Io ought to go towards the northwest instead of the south ; in the former, we have a harsh asyndeton, and violence is done to the natural obvious construction. For Salmydessus, comp. Antig. 969. —— γνάθος. This metaphor, according to one Scholiast, is derived from the perilous nature of the coast, the shallows and cliffs of which were destructive to vessels thrown upon them by northerly winds. The coast for 700 stadia went by this name, διὰ τὸ τοὺς εἰς

αὐτὴν πλέοντας καταναλίσκειν. Another deduces it from the form of the coast resembling a jaw. But Schütz under stands γνάθος more indefinitely of the *mouth* of the Propontis, called Salmydessian, because the coast known by that name extended to the Thracian Bosporus. —— The country of the Amazons was considered in Strabo's time (see 11. 5, § 1 – 3) to be in the mountains above Albania, or else under Caucasus towards the north. The poet places them farther to the south, and a set of fables settled them near the Thermodon. They guided Io *with great pleasure*, on account of her sex, but by what route it does not appear; perhaps around the Euxine.

729. ἰσθμόν. This Schütz understands, not of the Tauric Chersonese (now the Crimea) itself, but of the tongue of land between the Mæotis and the Euxine on the east of the former, where the mart of Phanagoria was built. On this scheme, Io went from Asia into Europe by crossing the strait named from her the Bosporus. In order to bring her back into Asia again, which v. 735 requires, Schütz takes her along the northern coast of the Euxine, and across the Thracian Bosporus into Asia Minor, and the next thing we hear of her is her arrival at Cisthene, near the ends of the earth. The improbability of this is manifest. Io passes from some European region into the Tauric Chersonese, swims the Bosporus, and is thus in Asia at once. The Tanis and Palus Mæotis were considered the boundary between Europe and Asia. Comp. Strabo 11. 1, § 1.

731. αὐλών, *a narrow channel*. The present name is the Straits of Kertch, or Jenicale.

743. αὖ, *in your turn*, as the Chorus did, v. 687. —— ἀναμυχθίζει, you *groan out*. Blomf. has noticed the simple μυχθίζω in but one passage, viz. Meleager's 52d Epigram. It is found also in Polyb. 15, § 26; Theocr. Idyl. 20, 13 The root is the sound μῦ, as Blomf. remarks.

747 – 750. τί — οὐκ ἔρριψα ἐμαυτὴν — ὅπως ἀπηλλάγην; *why*

did I not throw myself — so that I had been freed? ἵνα, ὡς, μή, more rarely ὅπως, are found with the aorist, or imperf. indic., when actions are spoken of which should have happened, but did not. Comp. v. 157; Œd. Rex 1389, 1392; and Mt. § 519.

754. αὕτη, sc. τὸ θανεῖν. It is put by attraction in the gender of the predicate.

760. See Kühner, § 312, R. 12.

761. τύραννα. The tragic poets often use τύραννος as an adjective of two endings. —— σκῆπτρα is in the accusative.

764. ἀσχαλᾷ. Comp. v. 303. —— τοιοῦτον ᾧ. Comp. Alcest. 194.

765. θέορτον = θεῖον.

766. τί δ' ὄντιν', sc. ἐρωτᾷς. —— ῥητὸν αὐδᾶσθαι, a kind of pleonasm for ἔξεστιν αὐδᾶσθαι, arising perhaps from a *confusio duaram locutionum*, viz. ῥητὰ τάδε and ἔξεστι, or δεῖ αὐδᾶσθαι τάδε. Comp. εὐδρακὴς λεύσσειν, Soph. Philoct. 847, and Schaefer's note; εὐμαθὴς κρῖναι, Æschin. c. Ctes.; φατὸν λέγειν, Aristoph. Av. 1713.

768. ἢ τέξεταί γε, *yes* by a wife *who will bear*, or *yes because she will bear*. For what is said, comp. v. 909.

770. Some MSS. have λυθῶ, but λυθείς, as a more exquisite reading, is preferred by the best critics. The discourse is interrupted by Io's inquiry. One may supply δείξω πῶς αὐτὴν ἀποστρέψει. Several editors, unwilling to admit an interruption of the discourse, supply ἀποστροφὴ ὤ. But Prometheus would call *what he should do*, rather than *himself*, an ἀποστροφή.

774. Hercules, who is here meant, was the thirteenth in descent from Io, through Danaus, Perseus, and others.

780. ἑλοῦ ἢ = ἑλοῦ πότερον. ἢ is often thus used in the epic style, but rarely in other kinds of composition. —— φράσω is in the subjunctive.

782. τούτων σὺ τὴν μὲν κ. τ. λ. = τούτων χαρίτων σὺ τὴν μὲν τῇδε, τὴν δ' ἐμοί.

8

786, 787. οὐκ ἐναντιώσομαι — γεγωνεῖν. See v. 627.

789. μνήμοσιν δέλτοις φρενῶν, *the mindful* or *recollecting tablets of the mind* = the memory. As we might say *the memorandum-book of the mind*. This metaphor was not uncommon. Comp. Furies 265 (275); Suppl. 176 (179); Soph. Philoct. 1325. The Δέλτοι were the folded halves of a square cut diagonally, and took their name from Δ.

790. By ῥεῖθρον the Cimmerian Bosporus seems to be intended, for the poet would naturally return to the point where he left off, v. 735. It is possible, however, that the poet had the Phasis in his mind, which, in a frag. of the Prometheus Loosed, he calls the boundary of Europe and Asia.

791. There is plainly a *lacuna* here, and some suppose that a number of lines is lost. This renders the jarring theories concerning the course of Io both possible and uncertain. It is not certain what sea is meant in the next line; Voss discovers it to be the Thracian Bosporus; Völcker, the Straits of Gibraltar. Perhaps it is the Caspian. Io might say of the critics, ποῖ, πόποι, ποῖ μ' ἄγουσι;

793. There is from this place onward a very wide division among scholars, as to the course of Io. Some in the present age, as Voss and Hermann, suppose that the poet conceived her path to be in a northward and then in a westward direction to Libya, where the most common opinion placed the Gorgons and Phorcides. Hermann indeed treats the opposite opinion, viz. that she went eastwardly to Æthiopia, with contempt (Opuscula, 4. 275); but notwithstanding, with Mannert (Geog. 4. 88), and Müller (Geschichte der Dorer, 1. 277), I accede to it as the best supported. Quite a thorough examination of this very difficult subject of Io's wandering is to be found in Völcker's Mythische Geographie (Leipz. 1832), who takes her to the west end of Europe and into Libya. —— Κισθήνη is called by Harpocration a mountain of Thrace, and he quotes from Cratinus a line

which sufficiently shows its remoteness: κἀνθένδ' ἐπὶ τέρματα γῆς ἥξεις, καὶ Κισθήνης ὄρος ὄψει. This word is an offence to those who think that Io takes a westward course. Voss changed it into Κυνήτης, and Völcker into Κυρήνης. The Scholiast transports the place into Libya or Æthiopia.

794. Hesiod (Theog. 270) mentions the Phorcides and Gorgons under the names of Γραῖαι (= δηναιαὶ κόραι in this passage) and Γοργοί. The latter dwelt near the Hesperides, beyond the ocean, on the confines of night. The former were gray-haired from birth, but of the other traits of the fable here mentioned the poet says nothing.

795. κυκνόμορφοι. "De canitie Stanleius interpretatur, nec ipse reperio quod melius sit." Schütz. The Scholiast understands this word literally. —— ἐκτημέναι, an Ionic form for κεκτημέναι, rarely found in Attic writers.

796. ἇς οὔθ' ἥλιος. The same is said of the Cimmerians by Homer, Odys. xi. 15.

799. δρακοντόμαλλοι, *having snakes for hair.* The word μαλλός, used properly of wool, stands also, according to Hesychius, for ἡ καθειμένη κόμη.

801. φρούριον seems to mean *thing to be guarded against.*

803–807. In the northern parts there was fabled to be abundance of gold, which the Arimaspi attempted to steal from the griffins that guarded it. To this Milton alludes, Par. Lost, ii. 943. Comp. Herodot. 4. 13 and 27, and 3. 116. The one-eyed Arimaspi were reputed to dwell next to the Issedones, who bordered upon the Scythians; next to them lived the griffins, and then the Hyperboreans upon the sea. Some poets transferred the Hyperboreans to the west of Europe; but I know of no good evidence that the abode of the Arimaspi was otherwise thought of, than as being to the north or northeast of the Scythians, except by the Scholiasts on this passage, who assign Cisthene, Arimaspi, Gorgons, and all, to Libya. The griffins also seem to be exclusively an Eastern fiction. We must suppose then, that the poet put the Gorgons in the remote east, which he migh do in conformity with one version of the fable. Comp. Schol. on Pind. 10. 72: αἱ δὲ Γοργόνες κατὰ μέν τινας ἐν τοῖς Ἐρυθραίοις μέρεσι καὶ τοῖς Αἰθιοπικαῖς ἅ ἐστι πρὸς ἀνατολὴν καὶ μεσημβρίαν, etc. And several other fables of a similar kind had a double locality in the eastern and western parts unknown.——κύνας. The griffins, like the Sphinx, Œd. Rex 391, the eagle, *infra* 1022, and the Furies, Choëph. 911 (924), are called *dogs*, from their being fierce and rapacious ministers of Jove, his hounds which he set upon men.——ὀξυστόμους, ἀκραγεῖς, were added to explain the metaphor in κύνας. The griffins were dogs only in figure, as they had the beaks of birds, and did not bark.——νᾶμα Πλούτωνος πόρου. Æschylus says equally πόρον Ἰσμηνὸν (Sept. ad Theb. 360), and πόρον Σκαμάνδρου (Choëph. 361). Comp. πόρον Ἅλυος ποταμοῖο, Persæ 848. The river derived its name from πλοῦτος, as abounding in gold-sand; and so Hades received the name of Pluto from his being lord of underground treasures. Those who lay the scene of these verses in the extreme west, understand this of Tartessus or Bœtis in the Spanish gold region.

807. It may be asked, how the poet could go at one leap from Northeastern Asia to Æthiopia, as though they were contiguous. The reply is, that the ancients in early times placed Æthiopia in the remote east, as well as in the west. In Odys. i. 23, we have

Αἰθίοπας, τοὶ διχθὰ δεδαίαται, ἔσχατοι ἀνδρῶν,
οἱ μὲν δυσομένου Ὑπερίονος, οἱ δ' ἀνιόντος.

And Herodotus (7. 70) speaks of the Eastern Æthiopians as an historical tribe. And then, as all between was an unknown land to the poet, he neither conceived of the great distance between the two regions, nor knew how to fill it up with details. It is not unlikely that he conceived of the Nile as running westward from that remote region; for Strabo informs us that Alexander, having found crocodiles

NOTES.

in the Hydaspes of India and Ægyptian beans in the Acesines, thought that he had discovered τὰς τοῦ Νείλου πηγάς, and for a time meditated sending a fleet down the stream into Ægypt (xv. 696).

808. πρὸς ἡλίου — πηγαῖς, i. e. where the sun rises. Soph. in a frag. speaks of νυκτὸς πηγάς, meaning the west. But the two examples are not entirely parallel. Voss understands this of the well-known fountain at the temple of Jupiter Ammon, which is called by Herodot. 4. 181, and by Diodor. xvii. 50, ἡλίου κρήνη.

811. Above the cataracts of the Nile, the Romans still called it Niger (= Αἰθίοψ) from the blackness of the waters of the blue river, or central branch.

814. μακρὰν ἀποικίαν, *remote colony*, i. e. distant from Greece; sc. Canopus. Comp. 846.

817. ἐπαναδίπλαζε, *fold over again, redouble*, hence, *repeat the question*.

822. που, *I think*.

827, 828. The sense is, *I will however omit the greatest part of what I could say* (λόγων), *and* (after proving my knowledge of the future from my supernatural knowledge of the past) *will proceed to the very close of your wanderings*.

829. ἐπεί. The apodosis begins with ἐντεῦθεν, v. 836.

830. αἰπύνωτον, *seated on a high ridge*.

831. θῶκος, Ionic for θᾶκος, which last appears in most MSS. in v. 280; but Well. reads θῶκον there also.

832. Render, *and* (where are) *the talking oaks, a wonder incredible*. Comp. Odys. xiv. 327; Soph. Trachin. 171; Herod. 2. 57. These oaks are called by Soph. and Herod. φηγοί, which were oaks bearing the best acorns, = *fagus* in Latin.

835. εἰ τῶνδε προσσαίνει σέ τι, *if aught of these things pleases you*. Spoken sarcastically, = for perhaps you like the high honor of being called Jupiter's wife. The reading

of the MSS. is ἔσεσθαι τῶνδε, but the elision ἔσεσθ', inadmissible though it may be, is necessary to the sense, for Wellauer's τί; will be approved by few. Dindorf, with reason, attributes this flat verse to an interpolator.

837. It is plain that what is here called the Gulf of Rhea is either the same with the Ionian Sea, or was the whole of that of which the Ionian was a part, viz. the sea between Greece and Italy. A probable derivation of the name *Ionian* is from the commercial visits of the Ionians to that quarter. — If the first ι in Ἰόνιος is long, as elsewhere, the word is made trisyllabic by synizesis. Comp. 680.

840. Part of the MSS. have κληθήσεται, *nomen accipiet*, instead of κεκλήσεται, *nomen geret*, as in the text. Griffiths.

843. πεφασμένου is from φημί.

846. ἐσχάτη χθονός, *on the borders of the land*, i. e. near the coast. So Eustathius cited by Stanley.

847. προσχώματι, the *deposit* or *made land* at the mouth of the Nile. The Schol. and Schütz understand it of the embankments collectively, on which the cities of the Delta stood, in order to be out of reach of the overflow.

849. ἐπαφῶν. Elmsley says on this verse, — " Displicet in hoc senario subita temporum mutatio, cum vel ἐπαφήσας vel θιγγάνων dicendum esset. Simile vitium infra 638, sustulit Blomf. Sed magnam licentiam in hac re sibi permittunt Tragici. Tale est κλύειν, ἀκοῦσαι, in Choëphorum prologo." In v. 637 (638) ἀποδύρεσθαι is still retained by Well. In the present line perhaps ἐπαφῶν, the present participle, is properly used on account of the continued act involved in the idea of *handling* or *stroking*, while θιγών, in the aorist, is used of the momentary one of *touching*. In the instance from Choëph. 5, cited by Elmsley, κλύειν may be a true aorist infinitive, since, as Buttmann remarks (largest Grammar 2. 170), ἔκλυον the imperfect is constantly so used. ἔτικτον and τίκτουσα, which seem at first sight to be used in an aorist sense, and were so explained in this note in the

first edition, are better accounted for by giving to τίκτω, when seemingly so used, the sense of *to be a parent*. —— ἀταρβεῖ, "*placidâ* a quâ nihil amplius mali timendum est," *in which there is nothing fearful.* Schütz. In this signification the compound follows ταρβέω in its rare sense of *frightening.*

850. γεννημάτων = γέννησις, sc. διὰ τοῦ ἐπαφῆσαι καὶ θιγεῖν. It depends on ἐπώνυμον. An elegant conjecture of Wieseler (Adversaria in Æschyl. Prom., etc., 1843) is γέννημ' ἀφῶν, i. e. an offspring named Epaphus after the handlings of Zeus. —— In vv. 851 and 869 we have τέξεις from τέξω, a rare form for τέξομαι.

853. πεντηκοντάπαις, *consisting of fifty children.* The fifty daughters of Danaus are meant.

854. ἐλεύσεται. This future is rare in Attic writers, who employ εἶμι instead of it.

855. θηλύσπορος = θήλεια, literally, *of the female sex by birth.* —— συγγενῆ γάμον ἀνεψιῶν, *marriage within the kindred with cousins.* See Antig. 793.

856. ἐπτοημένοι. πτοέω may be spoken of any agitating passion. Callim., H. in Dian. 191, cited by Blomf., says, πτοηθεὶς ὑπ' ἔρωτι, which is the passion meant here. Plato says (Repub. 439 D), ἡ ψυχὴ ἐρᾷ τε,— καὶ περὶ τὰς ἄλλας ἐπιθυμίας ἐπτόηται.

859. φθόνον σωμάτων ἕξει θεός = ὁ θεὸς φθονήσει (sc. τοῖς ἀνεψιοῖς, the sons of Ægyptus) σωμάτων αὐτῶν, i. e. shall be unwilling to give their persons into their cousins' hands.

860, 861. Πελασγία, sc. γῆ. Argos is so called by Æsch. throughout his play of the Suppliants, which relates to the Danaïdes here spoken of, and by the other tragic poets. See Spanheim on Callim., H. in Lav. Pal. 4. The Pelasgi occupied the north and east of Peloponnesus, before the Achæans, the people of epic poetry, came in from the north. —— δέξεται, sc. αὐτάς, the Danaïdes implied in σωμάτων. —— δαμέντων, κ. τ. λ., *they,* i. e. the sons of Ægyptus, *hav-*

ing been slain in female war through daring that kept watch by night. The daughters of Danaus agreed to kill their husbands by night, and all but one, Hypermnestra, did so. —— θηλυκτόνῳ Ἄρει, more literally, *Marte muliebri manu interficiente.* Elmsley supposes this passage to be corrupt.

863. δίθηκτον = δίστομον, ἄμφηκες. —— σφαγαῖσι, *throats,* properly the part of the body where the victim is struck by the slaughter-knife. The Etym. Mag. defines σφαγὰς by κατακλεῖδας, the hollow just above where the collar-bones are inserted in the breast-bone.

868. κλύειν, *audire, vocari.* Comp. Alcest. 961.

871. See v. 774.— γε μήν, *at least however,* i. e. know however thus much at least, that.

877. σφάκελος, *shooting pain, spasm,* or *twinge.* In v. 1046 this word denotes a *blast* or furious and irregular motion of wind. Comp. Eurip. Hippolyt. 1353, κατὰ δ' ἐγκέφαλον πηδᾷ σφάκελος. —— ὑπὸ θάλπουσι, *burn me within* = *subeunt et ardent.* The meaning *within,* here given to ὑπό, arises from its primitive meaning *under,* since that which has come under the roof of a house, or under the surface of the body, is within it. So ὑποδέχομαι means *I receive under my roof, within my house.* Comp. ἔθαλψεν ἄτης σπασμός, Soph. Trachin. 1082.

880. Hesychius defines ἄρδις by ἀκίς, *point, sting,* and cites this passage. Herodot. 4. 81, uses it with ὀϊστοῦ, of an arrow-head. —— ἄπυρος, Schol. πολύπυρος, Blomf. *ardentissimus,* as though α were intensive; but this is improbable, as not more than five or six fair examples of this use of α can be produced. See Buttmann's Largest Gram. 2. 358. Well. defines it *igni similis;* but the epithet would be too tame, if this were its meaning. Schütz translates it *sine igne factus,* as though there were an allusion to the physical meaning of ἄρδις. ἄπυρος ἄρδις then would be a weapon's point not made *by fire, which no smith has fashioned.* This is poetical, and in the style of Æschylus, who

occasionally explains by an epithet his own metaphors. Something so χρυσὸς ἄπυρος means *gold that has not passed through the fire.*

881. φρένα takes its physical meaning, *the diaphragm, præcordia.*

883. The figure in this and the next line denotes Io's inability to follow a *straight course* in her words, and is explained by the closing phrase, γλώσσης ἀκρατής.

885. " Significat," says Schütz, " querelas nihil adversus calamitatem proficere. *Fluctibus obloqui* pro *loquendo nihil proficere* nota est metaphora. Confer v. 1001." I doubt if the figure means any thing more than the preceding one, viz. that she talks confusedly through the influence of her pain. The successive stings of her frenzy are compared to waves tossing upon her, against which her words beat confusedly, i. e. which force them from her in wild disorder. So the Scholiasts explain it. εἰκῇ is not *frustra* here, but *temere, at random.*

887. The subject of the ode is the danger of being raised above one's condition, and is suggested by the relation between Jupiter and Io. Its spirit is the dread of superior power, and thus it ran in strong contrast with the feelings of Prometheus, and gave occasion to his speech, v. 908, seq.

890. κηδεῦσαι καθ' ἑαυτόν, *to form a marriage connection in one's own rank.* The wise man who conceived and broached this maxim was Pittacus, whom a young man came to consult whether he should marry a female of his own quality, but poor, or one above him, who was rich. Pittacus pointed to some boys that were whipping their tops, and said they would teach him. The young man drew nigh, and, hearing them say to their tops, τὴν κατὰ σαυτὸν ἔλα (sc. ὁδόν), took an omen from the words and married his equal. This is made the subject of a neat epigram by Callimachus, preserved in Diog. Laert. i. § 80, Vit. Pittaci.

891. διαθρυπτομένων, *who take airs upon themselves, act haughtily.*

897. ἀστεργάνορα = στυγάνορα, v. 724.

899. μέγα was first put for με γάμῳ here, which suited neither sense nor measure, by Schütz, whom Blomf. and others have followed.

900. δυσπλάνοις, comp. Antig. 1266, note, = δυστυχέσι here. —— Ἥρας, caused by Juno. For this relation of the genitive to nouns, see Mt. § 375. —— πόνων. This word is wanting in one MS. It is ejected from the text with γάμων in the strophe, which all the MSS. have, by Schütz, Porson, and Blomf. Hermann (De Epitritis Doriis, Opuscula, 3. 97) says, "Verissima et certissima est librorum scriptura, γάμων in fine addentium, cujusmodi vox addenda esset, etiam si nullus eam liber præberet." And his reason for so saying is, that the catalexis which takes place, when these words are omitted, is not a suitable or pleasant one. πόνων has the force of an adjective, e. g. of μοχθηροῖς.

901. The text of this and the next two lines is somewhat uncertain; and ἄφοβος in particular is suspicious, on account of the tautology. The order is ἐμοὶ δ' ὅτι μὲν ὁ γάμος (ἐστιν) ὁμαλός, (i. e. because I am married to one *on a level with myself,*) ἄφοβός εἰμι, οὐ δέδια. ὅτι μὲν forms a contrast to μὴ δέ, which two words should be written apart. The sense is, *But may no God,* &c. That event only could cause alarm. —— ἄφυκτον ὄμμα, *with look* or *eye not to be avoided.* ὄμμα is an accusative joined to an active verb of its own signification. Comp. Mt. § 421, Obs. 3; K. § 278. 2.

904, 905. The sense is, *This war is no war* (i. e. is an ineffectual one), *fruitful in difficulties: nor know I what would become of me.* Comp. Alcest. 51, 120, 153. The war meant is resisting the love of a God. πόριμος governs an accusative by its active force. See Antig. 787.—A noun often, as here, has joined with it a privative adjective from the same or a kindred root, which serves to deny the existence of the noun in its proper sense; as ἄγαμος γάμος, *a marriage that is no marriage*, an unhappy one; ἀμήτωρ μήτηρ, *a mother who is not such*, Electr. 1154. Of another kind are such expressions as δύσπονοι πόνοι, Antig. 1276; δύσπλανοι ἀλατεῖαι, 900 *supra*; τηλέπλανοι and πολύπλανοι πλάναι, 576, 585; where the meaning of the compound is determined chiefly by the first part of it.

908. οἷον may be resolved into ὅτι τοιοῦτον. Mt. § 480, Obs. 3. —— The marriage here meant is with Thetis. According to Pindar, Isthm. 8. 58 *seq.*, when Jove and Neptune were rival suitors of Thetis, Themis (and not Prometheus) foretold, " that it was fated that the sea-goddess should bear a son superior to his father, and who, if she were married to Jupiter or Neptune, κεραυνοῦ τε κρέσσον ἄλλο βέλος διώξει χειρὶ τριόδοντός τ' ἀμαιμακέτου." These last words resemble vv. 922 – 925, but are without the verbosity of those lines. This prophecy is conditional. Comp. v. 913.

910. ἄϊστον ἐκβαλεῖ = ἐκβαλεῖ ὥστε ἄϊστον εἶναι.

918, 919. The sense is, *These things will be of no assistance to him in regard to falling*, i. e. will not hinder him from falling. ἐπαρκέω adopts the construction of κωλύω as implying *prevention*. —— For πεσεῖν πτώματα, comp. Antig. 1046, and the Grammars.

924. γῆς τινάκτειραν νόσον, *the evil* or *plague that causes the earth to quake*. Earthquakes were ascribed to Neptune, because they are attended with the swelling and breaking of the sea upon the coast. Hence his name ἐνοσίχθων.

925. αἰχμήν, *sceptre*. Comp. v. 405.

928. θην = δή. This Homeric particle is hardly known to the tragic poets. —— ἐπιγλωσσᾷ Διός, *you went against* or *concerning Jove*.

934. The true reading here is probably τοῦδ' ἔτ' ἀλγίω, as Elmsley conjectured.

936. Adrasteia was a name of Nemesis, who punished undue pride. The verse is an exhortation to lay aside excessive stubbornness.

937. τὸν κρατοῦντ' ἀεί. ἀεί = *at any time*. Comp. Alcest. 700; Xen. Anab. V. 4. 15, VII. 5. 15.

938. The construction is ἐμοὶ μέλει Ζηνὸς ἔλασσον ἢ μηδέν, *I care less than nothing about Jupiter.*

943. πάντως (*certainly*) is taken with ἐλήλυθε.

946. πορόντα denotes the way in which the act of ἐξαμαρτόντα takes effect. *Who sinned — by procuring.*

950. αὔθ' ἕκαστα, *every thing as it is in itself*. This phrase may denote things *exactly as they are* without concealment or ambiguity, or things *in all their particulars*, as opposed to a summary. The first sense obtains here. —— μηδέ μοι διπλᾶς ὁδοὺς — προσβάλῃς, i. e. *nor* (through your ambiguity in telling what is required) *put upon me the necessity of taking two journeys* (from heaven), i. e. of coming again to ask an explanation.

952. τοῖς τοιούτοις, i. e. the crafty and disobedient, which qualities are implied in what Mercury forbids.

954. ὡς θεῶν ὑπηρέτου, *qualis deorum ministrum decet*, Schütz; *considering that it comes from a servant*, Blomf. But if this last were the meaning, the word θεῶν, which takes off the edge of the sarcasm in some degree, would not be added. Comp. v. 983.

957. δισσοὺς τυράννους. Ophion and Saturn, according to the Schol. For Ophion and Eurynome

"had first the rule
Of high Olympus, thence by Saturn driven
And Ops, ere yet Dictæan Jove was born."

So Milton after Apol. Rhod. I. 503. It is more probable, however, that Æschylus had in his mind Uranus or personified heaven, from whom and Gæa sprang Cronus or Saturn according to the Hesiodic mythology. The Ophion of an obscurer mythology may have denoted the same thing, the name being derived from the heavens surrounding the earth as a coiled snake.

961. The sense is, *Nay, I fall much and altogether short of it.*

966. The spirit of this reply is much like that of Satan to Gabriel. Par. Lost, iv. 970.

969. πατρὶ Ζηνὶ ἄγγελον, *a messenger* (not of my father, but) *of him whom you call father.* Comp. v. 947. It is said in scorn. But perhaps Prometheus uses the word πατήρ, as Kratos does vv. 4, 40, 53, as a perpetual title of Zeus.

976. εὖ παθόντες, *treated well* (by me). So Alcest. 810.

977. κλύω, *I perceive from what I hear.* —— μεμηνότα νόσον = μεμηνότα μανίαν. Comp. v. 919.

980. ὤμοι. As Schütz observes, this *one* expression of pain, forced from Prometheus, has a fine effect in showing the severity of his sufferings and the strength of his will. G. Schneider regards it less naturally as an expression of sorrow for the unthankfulness of the divinities. —— The sense of the line is, not that Jupiter has no pity, but rather that he knows no pain. —— In v. 981, ὁ γηράσκων χρόνος = *time as it grows old*, the progress of time.

985. καὶ μὴν — γε = *and surely;* but in v. 982 these particles = *and yet.* Comp. Alcest. 713. The sense is, *And surely, I might return him a favor, as I owe him one* (said in scorn). χάριν is to be supplied also after ὀφείλων.

986. This verse refers to the bitter irony of the preceding, which implied that Mercury was a child in supposing that Prometheus would do as he wished. —— παῖδα a Schol. explains by δοῦλον. But ἀνούστερος requires the other meaning, and παῖς in the sense of *servant*, being a word of familiar life, is not used by the tragic poets, except in calling out to porters, and on similar occasions. See Hermann on Antig. v. 1275 of his ed.

988. πευσοῦμαι seems to have coexisted with πεύσομαι, as φευξοῦμαι did with φεύξομαι.

999, 1000. τόλμησόν ποτε, *do but once summon the resolution*, or prevail over yourself. —— πρός, *in view of*.

1001. κῦμα is in the nominative. The sense is, *You trouble me in vain by your admonitions, as a wave* (would by its sound). So Morell and Butler. Schütz, Elmsley, and Blomf. make it an accusative. A parallel passage is then Eurip. Androm. 537: τί με προσπιτνεῖς ἁλίαν πέτραν | ἢ κῦμα λιταῖς ὡς ἱκετεύων.

1005. ὑπτιάσμασιν χερῶν, *supplications with the hands* (made by lifting up the hands with the back of them turned outwards).

1006. τοῦ παντὸς δέω. *I want the whole of it, I am without it altogether.* Comp. v. 961.

1007. The sense is, *It seems that, much as I may say, I shall even speak in vain.*

1011. σφοδρύνει. Schol. κομπάζῃ καὶ ἐπαίρῃ; rather, *you act violently* or *haughtily*. Blomf. has not found the word in any other classical author.

1013. μεῖζον is the MS. reading, which Well. retains, and interprets the clause thus: *pervicacia ipsa per se nihil*, vel potius *neminem*, superat. With most editors I have adopted Stanley's emendation μεῖον. —— μεῖον οὐδενὸς σθένει = *has less than no power, is utterly powerless.*

1016. ἔπεισι, *is coming, will come upon*. —— ὀκρίδα = ὀκριοέσσαν of v. 282.

1022. κύων. See the note on v. 803. —— For διαρταμησει in the next line, comp. Alcest. 494.

1023. σώματος μέγα ῥάκος, lit. *the great tatters of thy body* =, as Griffiths has it, *thy great mangled body.*

1024. πανήμερος. This word and πανημέριος seldom, if ever, have any meaning except *all day long;* and so a Schol., Blomf., and G. Schneider understand it. I think it better, however, with Schütz and Well., to interpret it *daily*, because *all day long* in itself means no more than *throughout one day*, and there is nothing in the context to extend the meaning. In a passage from the Prometheus Loosed, translated by Cicero, Tusc. Quæst. 2. 10, the poet speaks of the eagle as coming *every third day*, but it is not impossible for a poet to be inconsistent with himself. In καθημέριος *quotidianus* and *hodiernus*, there is an ambiguity of a somewhat similar kind.

1025. κελαινόβρωτον, *black to eat*, i. e. *black.* Comp. Alcest. 428. Blomf. translates *nigrum jecur victum præbens.*

1027. The fable was, that Chiron, the Centaur, thus took his place, and bore the penalty as his substitute. See Apollodor. ii. 5, § 4, and Heyne's note.

1031. λίαν εἰρημένος, *vehementer*, i. e. *serio dictus;* Blomf. καὶ augments the force of λίαν. So Eurip. Medea 526, ἐπειδὴ καὶ λίαν πυργοῖς χάριν; Odys. i. 46, καὶ λίαν κεῖνός γε ἐοικότι κεῖται ὀλέθρῳ. See Elmsley's Medea 513 (526), where the present passage is cited.

1033. τελεῖ, sc. Ζεύς, contained in Δῖον.

1037, 1038. The article with αὐθαδίαν, εὐβουλίαν, seems to denote a reference to the same words in vv. 1034, 1035.

1040. τοὶ = *be sure.*

1044. ἀμφήκης βόστρυχος πυρός, *the double-pointed curl*, or *twist, of flame.* The thunderbolt grasped in the middle by Jupiter was conceived to take at both ends the sinuous form of flame, which the Greeks compared to a lock of hair, to the beard, and the like.

1047. αὐταῖς ῥίζαις. See v. 221.

1049. ξυγχώσειεν. The reading of most authorities is ξυγχώσει ἐμέ. In this case we must make κῦμα a nominative, and join διόδους with Τάρταρον, the preposition being first used with the second noun. But on the one hand, the idea of mingling sea and sky is so natural, (see it repeated v. 1088,) and on the other, to speak of the body of Prometheus being thrown to the stars is so frigid, that ξυγχώσειεν — admitted into the text by Blomf., Well., and Schütz — is to be preferred. πνεῦμα is its subject and that of ῥίψεις but with θανατώσει perhaps Ζεύς is to be understood.

1051. ἄρδην, *raptim*, Well., *penitus*, Blomf. The word means, 1. *borne aloft*, as in Alcest. 608; 2. *borne away*, simply *away*, as here; 3. as the effect of being borne away, *utterly gone*, hence *entirely, outright*, a very common signification.

1054. For the construction, see Alcest. 760.

1056. μὴ παραπαίειν, i. e. ὥστε μὴ παραπαίειν, is another construction for τοῦ παραπαίειν, or, which is the same, τοῦ μὴ παραπαίειν. Comp. Alcest. 11.

1057. The MSS. vary exceedingly in the first part of this verse, and no various reading gives a good sense. Among the conjectures of learned men, I have allowed that of Dindorf, ἡ τοῦδε τύχη, to stand in the text, as the aptest and the least receding from the Medicean, — the best of the MSS., — which has εἰ τοῦδ' εὐτυχῇ. The sense is, *In what does his condition fall short of frenzy? What abatement has he in his madness?* Porson conjectured εἰ μηδ' ἀτυχῶν, Wellauer εἰ τῇδε τύχῃ, *if in this posture of his affairs*, Schömann, εἰ τάδ' ἐπαυχεῖ, *if so he boasts*.

1060. που, *somewhere*. This is used for ποι, as adverbs of rest often are, with verbs of motion, for adverbs of motion; because the final result of the action, viz. *rest*, is principally thought of. Thus μετά που χωρεῖτε = *go to some place where you may be in a retreat*. Adverbs of motion, on the contrary, are put where we should expect adverbs of rest; e. g. Choëph. 521, ποῖ τελευτᾷ λόγος, *in what direction does what was said end?* i. e. *what course* will it take to be fulfilled?—where motion is implied. But this is not always so.

1064. ὅ τι καὶ πείσεις, *such as you will* not only say, but also *induce* me to do.

1065. παρασύρειν. *præter necessitatem in medium proferre;* Well. *to drag along* or *forward*, hence *to introduce into discourse without occasion*, or *unsuitably*.

1079. εἰς after ἐμπλεχθήσεσθε adds the idea of motion to

the verb. The sense is, *Ye will be brought into, and entangled in*. Comp. Alcest. 841.

1080 – 1088. The trochaic verses of Pacuvius in Cicero de Orat. 3. 39, to which Blomf. calls attention, are worthy of being quoted here.

        Inhorrescit mare;
Tenebræ conduplicantur, noctisque et nimbum occœcat nigror;
Flamma inter nubes coruscat, cœlum tonitru contremit:
Grando mista imbri largifluo subita præcipitans cadit:
Undique omnes venti erumpunt, sævi existunt turbines:
Fervet æstu pelagus.

1089. ῥιπή, *the hurling of the thunderbolt*, or rather *the hurled thunderbolt itself*. With this word ἐπ' ἐμοὶ is to be joined, and means *against me*, or *at me*, as in v. 1043. ῥιπὴ ἐπ' ἐμοὶ διόθεν = βέλος ἐπ' ἐμοὶ ὑπὸ Διὸς ῥιφθέν.

1092. αἰθὴρ — εἱλίσσων. This is to be understood of the ether or upper sky, which, being the orbit in which the sun's revolutions are performed, is said to roll the sun around, as we say of a road that it conducts or carries a traveller to a certain place. Schömann, however, understands φάος of the light of *day*, born according to the Hesiodic Theogony with ether out of night. But how did ether roll the daylight around?

METRES.

94 — 100. Anapæstic dimeters.

114. A dochmius. $\smile \perp \overset{\prime}{\frown} \smile \overset{\prime}{\smile}$ (?) Comp. 566.
115. Bacchic tetrameter,
$\smile \perp \perp \smile \perp \perp \smile \perp \perp \smile \perp \perp$;
or this verse can be called two dochmii hypercatalectic. See Munk's metres, p. 127, and Hermann's Elementa, ed. Glasg., p. 187.
116. Iambic trimeter.
117. Dochmius and Pæon quartus (creticus),
$\smile \overset{\prime}{\frown} \perp \smile \overset{\prime}{\frown} \mid \overset{\prime}{\frown} \smile \smile$
See Herm., p. 170.
118, 119. Iambic trimeters.
120 — 127; 136 — 143; 152 — 159; 167 — 178; 186 — 192; anapæstic dimeters.

128 — 135 = 144 — 155.
Verse 1. Choriambic tetrameter. (Iambic dipodies in the first and third places.)
2. Choriambic tetrameter catalectic. (Iambic dipody in the first place.) The usual iambic catalexis. $\smile \perp \smile -, \perp \smile \smile \perp, - \smile \smile -, \smile \perp$.
3. Choriambic dimeter. (= first half of verse 2.)
4. Logaœdic dactylic. (2 dactyls, 2 trochees.)
5. = verse 3.

METRES. 103

6. Choriambic pentameter catalectic. (= verse 1, with an iambic catalexis added.)
7. Logaœdic dactylic with an anacrusis. (= verse 4, preceded by a short syllable.)

See Freese's Metrik, p. 305.

The general flow of these verses can also be made Ionic a minore, chiefly of the Anacreontic or broken sort. So Herm. (Elem., p. 314) and Dindorf (notes to Æschyl., v. 128), after a Scholiast.

159 — 166 = 178 — 185.
Verses 1–3, 5. Iambic dimeters. (The third foot of v. 2, and first of v. 5, are resolved.)
  4. Iambic trimeter. (The second, third, and fourth feet are resolved.)

  6. Dactylic penthemim.
  7 Trochaic penthemim. and dactyl. pentameter.

  8. Logaœdic dactyl. (Two dactyls, two trochees.)

Or to v. 7 a dactylic trimeter may be given, and to v. 8 four dactyls, two trochees. So Boeckh de Metris Pind. 138.

Initial *a* is long in ἀπαράμυθος, as in ἀθάνατος, when the metre requires.

277 — 297. Anapæstic dimeters.

397 — 405 = 406 — 414.
Verse 1. Ionic a minore dimeter (Anacreontic) preceded by an iambic penthemim.

  2. Two Ionic a minore dimeters, with one pure monometer interposed. (The text in the antistrophe is defective. The first dimeter was probably pure, so that δ' in the strophe injures

the metre. The second dimeter was an Anacreontic verse.)

3, 4. Consist each of two Anacreontics.

5. Ionic a minore dimeter. $\smile\smile\perp\perp\perp\smile\_\_$

(For this form see Munk's Metres, p. 150.) For the system see Herm. u. s., p. 314. These lines can be subjected to choriambic measurement. See Freese, p. 302.

415 — 419 = 420 — 424.

Verse 1 — 3. Trochaic dimeters.

4. Glyconean and logaœd. dactyl. (One dactyl, two trochees.) $\perp\perp, \perp\smile\smile\_\smile\perp \mid \perp\smile\smile\_\smile$

425 — 435. Epode of the foregoing.

Verse 1. Antispast and iambic tripody.

$\smile\perp\perp\_ \mid \smile\perp\smile\_\smile\_$

2. Dactylic trimeter catalectic in dissyllabum with anacrusis, followed by a trochaic dipody.

$\smile \mid \perp\smile\smile\_\smile\smile\_\_ \mid \perp\smile\_\_$

3. Dactylic trimeter catalectic in dissyllabum.

$\perp\smile\smile\_\smile\smile\_\_$

4. Iambic trimeter catalectic.

5. Dactylic trimeter catalectic in dissyllabum, followed by an ithyphallicus.

$\perp\smile\smile\_\smile\smile\_\_ \mid \perp\smile\_\smile\_\_$

6. Iambic dimeter.

7. Trochaic dimeter catalectic. $\perp\smile\_\smile\_\smile$

8. Iambic trimeter catalectic. (?)

$\smile\_\_\smile\frown\_\overset{\prime}{\frown}\smile\_\smile\_\_$

9. Dactylic tetrameter catalectic in dissyllabum, with a closing ithyphallicus, (?)

$\_\_\_\smile\smile\_\smile\smile\_\smile \mid \perp\smile\_\smile\smile;$

or dactylic tetrameter catalectic in syllabam, followed by an iambic dimeter catalectic.

METRES. 105

526 — 535 = 536 — 544.

Verse 1. Dactylic penthemim.
 2. Trochaic dipody and dactylic trimeter catalectic in dissyllabum.

  −́ ᴗ − − | −́ ᴗ ᴗ − ᴗ ᴗ − −

 3. = v. 2 with v. 1 appended.

  −́ ᴗ − − | −́ ᴗ ᴗ − ᴗ ᴗ − − | − ᴗ ᴗ − ᴗ ᴗ −

 4. = v. 2 closed by a creticus.

  −́ ᴗ − ᴗ | −́ ᴗ ᴗ − ᴗ ᴗ − − | −́ ᴗ −

 5. v. 1.
 6. Trochaic dimeter catalectic.
 7. Iambic dimeter catalectic.

If the text is entire, ἰδίᾳ in v. 543 must have its first ι long, owing to the force of the arsis; and the same is true of ἰσόνειρον, v. 549. Several edd. read ἐν ἰδίᾳ metri causá.

545 — 552 = 553 — 560.

Verse 1. Logaœdic anapæst. (Four anapæsts, iambic tripody catalectic.)

  ᴗ ᴗ −́ ᴗ ᴗ − ᴗ ᴗ − ᴗ ᴗ − ᴗ − −

 2. Logaœdic anapæst. (Two anapæsts, iambic dimeter catalectic.)   ᴗ ᴗ −́ ᴗ ᴗ − ᴗ − − −
 3. Logaœdic anapæst. (Two anapæsts, iambic dipody catalectic.)   ᴗ ᴗ −́ ᴗ ᴗ − ᴗ − −
 4. Trochaic dimeter.
 5. Logaœdic anapæst. (Four anapæsts, one iambus.)
 6. Dactylic tetrameter catalectic, with a closing trochaic dimeter.

  −́ ᴗ̆ ᴗ̆ − ᴗ ᴗ − ᴗ ᴗ − − | −́ ᴗ − ᴗ −́ ᴗ − −

561 — 565. Anapæstic dimeters.
566. Dochmius.   − −́ −̑ ᴗ −̆   (Last syllable short in exclamation.)
567 — 569. Iambic trimeters catalectic. (Omitting φοβοῦμαι in v. 569.)

570. Dochmiac dimeter.

571 = 567.

572. Dochmius hypercatalectic.

572, B. Dochmius and iambic dipody.

573. Iambus and dochmiac dimeter.

574 — 588 = 593 — 608. These lines were first noticed to be a strophe and antistrophe by Hermann.

Verse 1. Dochmiac dimeter.
    2. Creticus and v. 1. The last syllable of νόμον is produced, owing to the pause.
    3. Creticus, trochaic dipody (cretic dimeter hypercat.), dochmius. (See Seidler de Vers. Dochm., p. 128.)
    4, 5. (Unite these lines.) Three pæons quarti (i. e. cretic trimeter) and a dochmius.
    6. Cretic trimeter hypercatalectic.
    7. ἒ ἒ, two short syllables pronounced apart. Iambic tripody catalectic (iambic monometer hypercatalectic) and dochmius. See Herm. pp. 165, 166.
    8. Iambic dimeter catalectic. This should be closely joined to the preceding line. (Seidler, p. 164.)
    9. Dochmiac dimeter.
    10. Creticus, dochmius. (With the last syllable short in the antistrophe in exclamation.)
    11. Trochaic tripody. (Ithyphallicus.)

METRES.

  12. Trochaic tripody catalectic.
  13. Iambic dimeter.
  14. Iambic trimeter.
  15. = verse 11.
  16. Dochmius and cretic dimeter.

687 — 695. Epode of the foregoing. (Herm., p. 502)
Verse 1. Two pæons quarti (Herm., p. 171), i. e. cretic dimeter.
  2. Creticus, dochmiac dimeter.
  3. Dochmius.
  4. Iambic trimeter catalectic.
  5, 6. According to Seidler, p. 33, these lines consist of three dochmii with a dactyl prefixed. (?)
   $-\overset{\frown}{\_}\ |\ \_\overset{\frown}{\_}\ \_\cup\_,\ \_\_\_\_\_,\ \_\_\_\_\_$
  7. Iambus prefixed to dochmius hypercatalectic. (?)
   $\cup\_\ |\ \cup\_\_\cup\_\cup$
  8. Dochmius and iambic penthemim.
   $\cup\_\_\cup\_\ |\ \cup\_\_\cup\_\_$

742. $\cup\_\_\_,\ \cup\_.$ Antispast and iambus

877 — 880. Anapæsts.

887 — 893 = 894 — 900.
Verse 1. Dactylic penthemim. $\_\cup\cup\_\cup\cup\_$
  2. Trochaic dipody and two dactylic trimeters catalectic in dissyllabum.
   $\_\cup\_\_\ |\ \_\cup\cup\_\cup\cup\_\ |\ \_\cup\cup\_\cup\cup\_$
  3. = the first two parts of v. 2, closed by a creticus, = v. 531.
  4. Iambic penthemim and dactylic do. (Called iambelegus.)
  5. Trochaic dipody, and dactylic penthemim.

PROMETHEUS.

Verses 4, 5, 6, are remarkable for the rhyme in both strophe and antistrophe.

6. Trochaic trimeter catalectic.

— ◡ — — — ◡ — — — ◡ —

901 – 906. Epode of the foregoing.

Verse 1. Iambic dimeter. ◡ — ◡ ⌣ ◡ — ◡ ⌣

2. Dochmius, trochaic dimeter catalectic.

◡ — ◡ — ◡ — , — ◡ — — ◡ — (?)

3. Iambic trimeter catalectic.

◡ — ◡ — — ◡ — ◡ — — ◡ —

4, 5. Iambic trimeter (to οὐδ' inclusive), with all the syllables resolved except the last, followed by iambic dimeter catalectic.

6. Trochaic dimeter catalectic. — ◡ — ◡ — ◡

7. Logaœd. dactyl. — ◡ ◡ — ◡ ◡

Vv. 1, 2 united (excluding θεῶν) Boeckh on the critical treatment of Pindar, Berl. Trans. for 1822 – 23, p. 283; thus exhibits:

◡ — , — ◡ ⌣ ◡ ⌣ ◡ ⌣ ◡ — | — ◡ — ◡ — ◡

Two trochaic clauses preceded by an iambus as basis.

1036 — 1093. Anapæstic dimeters.

[PROMETHEUS.]

REFERENCES
TO
HADLEY'S GRAMMAR.

Verse 14, § 767. —— 16, σχεθεῖν, § 411. —— 21, § 882. —— 46. Comp. § 772. —— 62, § 802. —— 68, § 756, a. —— 86, § 544, c. —— 121, § 629, d. —— 145. Comp. § 523, b. —— 156–7, § 7.1, b; § 742. —— 213, § 736. —— 217. Comp. § 776, end. —— 221, § 604. —— 251, § 556. —— 268, § 775, b. —— 269, § 412, b. —— 284, § 551. —— 285, § 509, b. —— 317, see v. 251. —— 330. Comp. § 801, a. —— 354, last l., § 602. —— 388, § 677. —— 389, § 544, c. —— 402, § 552. —— 406, § 547, c. —— 433, § 569. —— 464. Comp. § 587, a, § 595, c. —— 564, ποινάς, § 501. —— 584, § 577, a. Comp. § 544, b. —— 594, § 826. —— 621, § 777. —— 626, see v. 584. —— 627, § 817, b. —— 628, § 428, 8. —— 658, § 641, a. —— 659, § 740, a. —— 660, § 826. —— 667. Comp. §§ 734, 736. —— 683, § 698. —— 712, πελάζειν, § 602, 1, § 784. —— 714. Comp. § 590 a. —— 749, § 742. —— 754. Comp. § 513. —— 760. Comp. § 795, e. —— 795, ἐκτημένοι, § 319, D, end. —— 808, § 551, § 514, c. —— 854, § 450, 2, a. —— 900, § 569. —— 903, § 547. —— 908. Comp. § 815. —— 918, § 847. —— 919, § 547, a. —— 921, § 674. —— 966. Comp. § 578, b. —— 977, § 547, b. —— 988. Comp. § 377. —— 1006, § 575, a. —— 1079, § 618, a.

www.ingramcontent.com/pod-product-compliance
Lightning Source LLC
Chambersburg PA
CBHW020120170426
43199CB00009B/578